THE BUSINESS OF GENEROSITY

*HOW COMPANIES, NONPROFITS, AND
CHURCHES ARE WORKING TOGETHER
TO DELIVER REMARKABLE GOOD*

dr. stephen r. graves

The Business of Generosity
Published by KJK Inc. Publishing
P.O. Box 9448
Fayetteville, AR 72702

Details in some anecdotes and stories have been changed to protect the identities of the persons involved.

ISBN [[978-1-940794-00-6]]

Copyright © 2014 by Dr. Stephen R. Graves

Prepared in association with Edit Resource, LLC (*editresource.com*)

THE BUSINESS OF GENEROSITY
*HOW COMPANIES, NONPROFITS, AND CHURCHES ARE
WORKING TOGETHER TO DELIVER REMARKABLE GOOD*

PREFACE

GENEROSITY IS NOW big business, full of best practices and category leaders. It includes money, acts of kindness, and branded goodwill. Organizations of many sorts, including some never-before-seen types, are fueling generosity's growth. Annual reports covering every industry, and touching every corner of the globe, highlight the equivalent of a "generosity index" for us to benchmark and measure success against. Generosity is now standard language on both sides of every street.

The business of generosity is also an expected common thread in most books on philanthropy, business, or global ministry strategy. Two recent examples: philanthropy strategist Laura Arrillaga-Andreesen, in *Giving 2.0*, talks of the convergence where "charity meets a business model"; and Howard G. Buffett, son of the Sage of Omaha, explores the new edges of social impact in *40 Chances*[1]. A week doesn't go by that every major news outlet isn't highlighting an emotionally charged generosity story. Even ESPN's *GameDay* has shifted its editorial grid to include heartwarming stories of human help every Saturday during its college football special.

Trendwatching.com terms the living generation as "Generation G" (for *generosity*, not *greed*)[2]. Generosity is simply pervasive.

One expression in the generosity uptick is the attention to *cause*. In fact, cause is on a rampage (a good kind of rampage). It is hard to find a business or church that hasn't folded the concept of cause into its core offering. Big-name personalities are pitching their cause of choice, individuals are branding themselves with their causes, and there is an entire economy dedicated to directing goodwill around the earth.

With this cause and that cause and the other cause always in sight, the generosity tide is rising.

Or is it?

Is generosity really in growth mode, or is there just more giving noise? Are companies authentically evolving their business models for organic generosity, or is generosity just a trendy marketing storefront? Are we really more generous as a people, or have we just become skilled traders—"If I do this for you, what can I get back for it?" Is my inner motivation primarily tied to gaining a stronger brand to pitch investors or donors or to getting a leg up on the competition? Is it sustainable or even smart to put a pair of shoes on every barefoot child?

Or does sustainability even matter when it comes to caring for those in need? And the list of questions goes on.

I'll be exploring some of the regions of skepticism later in *The Business of Generosity*. But one thing is beyond question: the generosity dialogue has been dialed up.

I point out in this book that generosity is something that both for-profit and not-for-profit organizations are intensely interested and active in these days. I understand both sides. I have been an entrepreneur, a business executive, a coach for leaders of corporations and NGOs, an impact investor, a board member, a church leader, and a student and observer of organizational and generational trends. I like to think this background gives me a unique perspective on the spread and evolution of generosity. This book is the harvest of the best of what I've learned in this area.

And now about the title. *The business of generosity* is the term I use to frame the entire process or ecosystem of generosity, starting with the heart of the matter, reaching through the most innovative of generosity channels, and eventually touching those points of our neighborhood and world that are most in need of help.

"THE GENEROSITY DIALOGUE HAS BEEN DIALED UP. "

It's the whole picture of generosity, encompassing all the organizations that are doing good for society as either a part or the whole of their mission.

For this project on the business of generosity, I engaged two-dozen rich conversations with experts in this field from around one touch point or another. (For their bios, see the back of the book.) Those conversations uncovered fresh insights and new models. They revealed some trends and even anticipated what's around the bend. The fact is, not only is generosity big business now, but also its ground rules seem to be in flux. Here are a few sample insights that came out of my conversations:

- "People want to sponsor a fifty-dollar goat rather than give us fifty dollars to keep the home office lights on," one leader of a local not-for-profit said.
- "The old label of business being coldhearted and all about profit is being deconstructed by necessity," said another friend.
- "The concept of investing and donating are sliding closely into the same swim lane" was another comment.

+ "Since everyone is now cause centered, what is the new means of differentiation?" asked a young leader who sits at the nexus of branding and cause.

In choosing to write *The Business of Generosity*, I wanted to share these insights and many more covering the generosity waterfront. My hope is that the ideas that lie ahead will allow you a faster spool-up as you pivot your thinking toward new horizons of care and revenue. I want to help provide clarity and confidence regarding the *what is* and the *what will be* of generosity, whether you're leading a business, a church, or a not-for-profit, or you're a one-person generosity campaign.

In five chapters, I hang my thoughts on the pegs of five overarching principles, each chapter concluding with a list of questions for you to think about on your own or discuss with someone you're on a generosity journey with. Then I end our conversation by getting practical with some quick guides in four specific generosity channels. As always, my voice is from the street back rather than the classroom out. My unbending bias for productive action seeps into the pages. And in fact, a make-it-happen mentality may be more important in this area than any other. Because this isn't a game. The needs of people around the world are real and urgent, and how we respond to them will help to determine the future of the human race.

There's a whole business of generosity out there to help. It's up to us to figure out where and how we can best join in.

"THE NEEDS OF PEOPLE
AROUND THE WORLD ARE REAL
AND URGENT, AND HOW WE
RESPOND TO THEM WILL HELP TO
DETERMINE THE FUTURE OF
THE HUMAN RACE."

CHAPTER 1

THE CURRENCIES OF GENEROSITY

Generosity is deeper than money and wider than philanthropy.

WHEN I WAS thirteen, my neighbor Mr. Cherry wanted his lawn mowed once a week. It wasn't that the grass grew more quickly on Mr. Cherry's yard than anywhere else in Biloxi, Mississippi, but who was I to argue? As a budding teenager whose sole source of income came from cutting grass (once every two weeks for most customers), I needed all the business I could get. Once a week was what Mr. Cherry wanted, and once a week was what he got, whether the lawn needed it or not.

Usually when I showed up to mow the grass, Mrs. Cherry welcomed me with a snack. (You can't mow on an empty stomach, right?) And when I finished mowing, Mr. Cherry would come out and walk the lawn with me, pointing out such things as how I did a good job of trimming close to the flowerbed without damaging the flowers. If I came up short somehow, he'd point that out, too, and explain how I could have done it better. In the end he sometimes gave me a small bonus for my good work. Not a bad gig for a thirteen year old.

I was confused, though, one day when I happened to notice a nearly new lawn mower in Mr. Cherry's garage.

If he had that prime piece of grass-shortening equipment at hand, why did he need me and my beat-up old push mower? I didn't understand it, but soon the question faded from my mind.

Years later, Mr. Cherry's motives in hiring me became clearer to me. Sure, he enjoyed having a freshly cut, well-manicured lawn acquired without raising a bead of his own sweat, but he also knew that the boy from a couple of streets over who did the mowing came from a single-parent family that didn't have much money. Bigger still, he saw some potential in the skinny kid who knocked on his door one day asking for summer work.

"GENEROSITY HAS FOR TOO LONG BEEN TOO NARROWLY BRANDED AS REFERRING TO WEALTHY PEOPLE GIVING AWAY FRACTIONS OF THEIR FORTUNES."

Mr. Cherry was, of course, giving me an income. But he was also giving me mentorship in doing a good job as a businessman (or businesskid, as was the case at the time). And he was giving me, at least for a short time once a week, a father figure in my life. Because he was a kind man, he was being generous to me in multiple lanes.

MONEY AND MORE

We tend to think that generosity is all about money. We hear "giving" and we think about a cash gift or perhaps some other material transfer, such as in-kind donations. We think about tithing, about foundation grants, about microlending, about child sponsorship checks, about pallets of relief supplies paid for by $10 texts to the Red Cross. And generosity does include all of that.

But the truth is, generosity is deeper than money and wider than philanthropy. It is more than just writing a check or dropping your loose change in a can called Help. It isn't best measured in transactions completed or numbers reached.

Just as there are many economic currencies around the world—dollars and dinars, pounds and pesos, yens and yuans—so there are many "currencies" of generosity. What are they? Well, there is the currency of giving one's time. The currency of physical energy. The currency of wisdom sharing. And that's not all. How about the currency of listening? The currency of empathy for those in pain? The currency of willingness to share one's connections and network with another?

The borders of generosity extend way beyond the confined precincts of money. One thing this means—and be thankful for it—is that generosity isn't only for the rich.

In my view, generosity has for too long been too narrowly branded as referring to wealthy people giving away fractions of their fortunes. We may not have much money, but we can volunteer to teach literacy to immigrants or swing a hammer for Habitat for Humanity. We may not have much money, but we can seed a reclaimed prairie, distribute blankets to the shivering homeless, or drive the elderly to doctor appointments. As my good friend Mike Rusch of Pure Charity recently reminded me, "It is the requirement of everyone to participate in some way."

Linguistic historians tell us that the word *generosity* has evolved from meaning "of noble birth" to referring to a nobility of spirit revealed in open-handedness toward others.[3] Generosity is not a case of *noblesse oblige* but a democratic potential open to us all.

Generosity conceived only in terms of excess funds given away by the affluent, then, is too limited. It's also dangerous. And it's one reason why the word *charity* has acquired a distasteful flavor in the mouths of many people.

Social entrepreneur Muhammad Yunus describes charity this way in *Banker to the Poor*:

> When we want to help the poor, we usually offer them charity. Most often we use charity to avoid recognizing the problem and finding the solution for it. Charity becomes a way to shrug off our responsibility. But charity is no solution to poverty. … Charity allows us to go ahead with our own lives without worrying about the lives of the poor. Charity appeases our consciences.[4]

Generosity isn't just about giving away a portion of our cash. "It's about an attitude, a lifestyle, a posture of living," Greg Spencer of The Paradigm Project told me. It is something that both originates organically and permeates every facet of our life.

Another friend, social entrepreneur Jeff Shinabarger, goes so far as to say, "Money is the last part of generosity. If you had no money, you could still be known and branded as a generous person."

But there's a big *nevertheless* that goes with all this.

Although generosity is more than financial, nevertheless there is a good reason why we usually link generosity with money in our thinking. Many times, it's money that creates possibilities for other things to happen. For example, if we've got cash in our wallet, it gives us the opportunity to buy a meal for a hungry person we meet on the street. A company that's turning a profit is more apt to spend money on its own people and causes that come its way. A church that's in the black at the end of its fiscal year has a greater chance to direct extra support to its missions.

We would be unrealistic to think money isn't a very important form of generosity currency. But we'd be myopic to think that the only currency of generosity is money.

VOLUNTEER NATION

On a visit to the West Coast one time, I heard Matt Emerzian, formerly an ambitious player in the music business, tell me his story of what happened when he drifted into the gravitational pull of helping others. It started when he was doing marketing/promotional projects for the likes of Coldplay, Avril Lavigne, and Bono, and then he inexplicably began having panic attacks.[5] His therapist showed him the first line of Rick Warren's book *The Purpose Driven Life*: "It's not about you." Then she told him to start helping others.

To say that he was resistant to the advice at first would be to put it mildly. Nevertheless, he did what his therapist had suggested, going to poorer neighborhoods and picking up litter, painting over graffiti, and such. Eventually it clicked.

Not only did he become a happier and more content person by taking his focus off himself and putting it on others who were less fortunate, but also he began to understand how much all of us, if we work together, can change the world for the better. He was motivated to write a book called *Every Monday Matters*, describing fifty-two down-to-earth strategies for making a difference each Monday of the year.[6]

He still practices regular acts of kindness toward others, and I still love hearing about it.

Emerzian was hooked by volunteerism. He's far from the first.

America has a volunteering tradition unique among the nations, as has been noticed since Alexis de Tocqueville famously called us "a nation of joiners" in social enterprises. The tradition continues today ... and seems to be expanding. According to U.S. government statistics,

- In 2011, the number of volunteers reached its highest level in five years, as 64.3 million Americans volunteered through an organization, an increase of 1.5 million from 2010.
- Americans volunteered a total of almost 8 billion hours, an estimated economic value of roughly $171 billion.
- A majority of Americans assisted their neighbors in some way and more than a third actively participated in a civic, religious, or school group.[7]

Americans give away around $300 billion dollars every year through corporate giving, foundation giving, and private giving.[8]

If the government statistics about the value of American volunteerism in 2011—$171 billion—is correct, then volunteerism contributes more than half as much economic value as do financial donations. And volunteerism offers the personal connection that giving away your cash inevitably lacks. Volunteerism is a powerhouse however you measure it.

I think of volunteerism as encompassing all of the nonmonetary aspects of generosity. In the biggest sense, volunteering is everything you do in a more personal way than writing a check to help others. What this means is that the dimensions of your bank account are not all that matter to your generosity. So do the dimensions of your heart.

All of us, whether we've been working in generosity a little or a lot, need to stop from time to time and gauge what's happening inside our hearts.

RETURN TO YES

Sasha Dichter, chief innovator of the Acumen Fund, helps to invest money entrepreneurially around the world to alleviate poverty. Philanthropy, in other words, is his job, and few are better at it. But on the way to work one day he began to question whether, despite his professional role, he truly was a generous person.

At a train station, a homeless man asked Sasha for a handout, and Sasha said no. This was his standard response in this sort of situation. He understood that panhandlers usually turn around and convert cash donations into the booze or drugs they are addicted to. So it would seem that the smarter move is not to give money directly to a panhandler but instead to support a program that provides help to the homeless. *But maybe there was something more to it than that*, Sasha thought. He started recalling all the no's he had been saying to people of late. Was *no* becoming who he was? It wasnt always that way. He wanted to get back to a place of *yes*.

"This wasn't about the smartest investgift I could give," he says. "This was about me. I wanted to stop saying no.

"As someone who works at a groundbreaking nonprofit as a fundraiser, as someone who thinks that the world is broken and in need of healing, and as someone who wanted to tap into my own motivations for doing this work, I felt like I needed to break this habit.

"I was hiding behind what was smart, and it was keeping me from doing what was right."[9]

Generosity isn't just about what you do. It's about who you are. If it's authentic, it springs from an inner source of compassion that feeds directly into your identity. Generosity not only sees and empathizes with a need, but it also moves to meet that need. It's what St. Augustine described as mercy: "heartfelt sympathy for another's distress, impelling us to help him if we can."[10]

In Jesus' story of the Good Samaritan, the Samaritan was not a field representative for the Jericho Social Venture Fund. He wasn't doing a job assigned to him by the Judean Department of Emergency Medical Services. He hadn't waited for a lengthy approval process by a patient advocacy group before he acted. He was apparently just an ordinary businessman on a foot commute who happened to come across a fellow commuter who had been robbed and beaten up.

Sad as the fellow's situation obviously was, the Samaritan didn't have to do anything about it—he could have turned his head and cruised on by. There was precedent for that. But "when he saw him, he took pity on him" (Luke 10:33).

The Greek word translated *pity* here referred to the inner organs.

Is there not something visceral in all of humanity that hurts when we see others in pain and broken? Well, we might say that something deep in this Samaritan's guts responded to the mugging victim's plight. His intrinsic pity leaped over their cultural divide, ripped up his agenda for the day, and loosened his grip on his personal resources. Faced with another's need, he said yes, of course, right away, whatever it takes, as long as it takes, yes, yes, yes.

Generosity is best described as a quality of personhood. Before it's a matter of giving or of doing, it's a matter of being.

If our actions don't originate from that internal place, if they aren't marked by compassion stretching from ourselves to another, then they are merely mechanical transactions. Such actions may provide a temporary balm; they may achieve some short-lived good; but they rarely, if ever, have the impact that heartfelt generosity is capable of achieving.

"The idea of being generous has been one of the key motivators in understanding what the next move for me will be," brand consultant Lane Wood says. "I can always strive to be the most generous person in the room with my words, with my time. It's less about what I'm doing or what I'm building right now as it is about who I'm becoming."[11]

Lately I've heard about a developing new niche for "generosity coaches"—people who teach others how to give. The interesting thing is, most of these coaches don't just teach the principles of strategic philanthropy or mentor social entrepreneurs through charitable start-ups. They also deal with the heart, helping clients to fan the fire of compassion in their hearts, purify their motives for doing generosity, and find and pursue the God-given passions lying within them.

You may or may not need a generosity coach. But you do need to stop from time to time and ask yourself if today you're a person of *yes* or not.

And so does your organization.

THE CHARACTER OF AN ORGANIZATION

If generosity is a quality of personhood, that begs a question: what does it mean to affirm that an organization— say, a business with a giving plan, a do-gooder nonprofit, or a church with an outreach to the community—is generous?

Is it absurd to even make the assertion? Can an organization be known for its generosity? Can an enterprise develop a "culture" of generosity?

When it comes to business, there are some who argue that we should flip the term *cause marketing* and make it *marketing cause* (emphasis on the *marketing*) because, when for-profit businesses engage in service to a cause, they are really just doing it as another way to make money. The theory goes, it may wind up doing some good, but the primary impetus isn't altruistic. It's essentially artificial—a put-on display that has little to do with what the company is really all about.

I see the issue. And insincerity is certainly a gaping pitfall in this area—we'll be getting to that more in the next chapter. Still, I believe that the attitude of generosity can be grafted into an entire family, community, or corporation.

When a bunch of people who have a generous lifestyle, a reputation for serving the social good, and credibility in the generosity sphere aggregate under a rooftop, their corporate identity can be known for generosity in a public and meaningful way.

I think of it this way: it's like how a person develops a character.

Historically, the word *character* refers to an engraved mark.

An individual's character is established by his or her habits and practices over a period of time, just as repeated etching in metal or wood will create a groove. If I want to be known as a man of honesty, then I need to make the decision to be honest over and over again. After repeated strokes, an image appears—the condition of honesty. A pattern or character is etched.

"CAN AN ORGANIZATION BE KNOWN FOR ITS GENEROSITY? CAN AN ENTERPRISE DEVELOP A 'CULTURE' OF GENEROSITY?"

The science of neuroplasticity would support this assertion, as it suggests that choices and habits actually create new neural pathways in the brain. I actually become different by what I choose to focus on. And so if I practice honesty repeatedly, you'll look up one day and see that I'm an honest man.

The same kind of thing happens within an organization.

If the leaders reinforce the conditions that encourage employees to work hard, for example, then it will be known as a hardworking organization. Or an organization can have a creative character. Or a relaxed character. Or whatever the group's leaders are aiming for. An organization can also have a generous character if it practices generosity consistently over a period of time in how it treats people, how it treats the planet, what its values are, how it delivers its offering, and so on. The image of generosity appears in time, and it is not artificial but true to life. It becomes part of our corporate culture or corporate character.

TAKERS, TRADERS, AND GIVERS

In economic terms, there are three roles any one of us might be playing at any particular time:

- *takers*—people who unfairly appropriate for themselves what belongs to others
- *traders*—people who exchange goods or services for money or some other consideration
- *givers*—people who see a need in others and try to meet it from their own resources

I think we can all agree that being a taker is a bad thing. But here is what I have noticed.

There isn't a lot of in-your-face taking going on in our society. If we saw an obvious taker, we would want nothing to do with him or her. Or we might even blow the whistle on the thief.

I think, when it comes to generosity, there are a lot of traders at hand. Now, I am not referring to the honest exchange between two open-eyed parties bartering for something.

I am talking about a devious, self-centered trader who is only trying to get something.

It is the polished and skilled art of giving something (think a compliment) *to* you in order to get something *from* you. The motive and agenda is fully about *me*.

You see, we live in a transactional world: "I'll do *this* for you if you'll do *that* for me. And beware, if you haven't done enough for me lately, then I'll have to stop doing things for you." There is an invisible seesaw of mutual benefit going up and down in every relationship. This happens in personal relationships. It gets pushed into business relationships too.

Some organizations are out for what's in their own interest regardless of what it does to someone else.

You could argue that this is what happens when Big Pharma markets life-saving drugs only in affluent nations, or when a corporation destroys irreplaceable natural resources to get low-cost raw materials, or when retailers gouge customers by raising prices during a crisis. This is the opposite of the business of generosity. It's the business of selfishness.

That's one of the things that gives cause marketing a bad name. "Marketing by any other name is still marketing."

When the better angels of our nature are in the ascendancy, transactions don't have to be the basis of our relationships in the world. Generosity can become the basis of our influence.

EVERYBODY'S BLIND SPOT

Tim Keller, founding pastor of the influential Redeemer Presbyterian Church in New York City, says,

> As a pastor I've had people come to me and confess that they struggle with almost every kind of sin. Almost. I cannot recall anyone ever coming to me and saying, "I spend too much money on myself. I think my greedy lust for money is harming my family, my soul, and people around me." Greed hides itself from the victim. The money god's modus operandi includes blindness to your own heart.[12]

What do you do if you realize you have been blind to your own greed? You open up your hand. You move to a posture of giving and releasing what you own and want and have.

You say *amen* to the plea of Basil the Great, who challenged early Christians to remember: "The bread in your cupboard belongs to the hungry man who needs it; the shoes rotting in your closet belong to the man who has no shoes; the money which you hoard belongs to the poor. You are not making a gift of your possessions to the poor man; you are handing over to him what is his."[13]

Don't trade. Give! Help out a friend with no calculation of what you get back. You'll find that giving has immaterial benefits that even the greatest trading deal can't match.

When a whitewater rafter is caught in a suck hole on the backside of a rock, he must act counterintuitively. To survive, he must remove his life vest and allow the rushing, foaming water to thrust him to the river bottom. Only then can he get a firm footing to shoot through the death loop all the way to the surface. Any other move will render the swimmer dead.

Being generous is the counterintuitive move that rescues us from the doom loop of self-interest and autobiographical living. So may you give of your wealth and give of yourself. May the organization you're associated with be free with all the currencies of generosity in its grasp.

"BEING GENEROUS IS THE
COUNTERINTUITIVE MOVE THAT
RESCUES US FROM THE DOOM
LOOP OF SELF-INTEREST AND
AUTOBIOGRAPHICAL LIVING."

1. Why are we sometimes too narrow in our definition of generosity?

2. See if you can name ten different kinds of generosity.

3. What is your default currency of generosity—money? volunteering? gifts? Which is most difficult, and why?

4. What can cause us to become calloused or blinded to the needy around us? Have you become a *no* person, or have you always been a *no* person? Why?

5. How has your upbringing shaped your thinking on generosity?

6. Do you think it is really possible for a company culture to become generous? Why or why not?

7. Who is part of your generosity narrative (those people who pushed generosity into your life story)?

8. Describe a non-monetary instance of generosity that impacted you.

9. What role do the heart and personal contentment play in your own generosity?

10. Have you met someone who is both a generous person and an unhappy person, an anxious person, or an angry person?

CHAPTER 2

THE GENEROSITY BRAND

*Generosity has become a powerful force
that knows no borders.*

SOMETIMES A PRODUCT or product line is a brand. (Cheez Whiz.) Sometimes a whole company is a brand. (John Deere.) And sometimes a brand is even larger than that—it's a *concept* that crosses organizational and international borders. In this sense, Christmas is a brand. Baseball is a brand. Fast food is a brand. No individual or corporation exclusively owns these brands, yet as concepts they are instantly understood and have the same rallying effect as other brands.

Generosity is a concept brand too. No church, no government assistance program, no foundation or charity, no corporate giving department, no high-net-worth donor owns generosity. But they each recognize it, participate in it, and promote it to others.

The generosity brand doesn't need a logo, a color scheme, or a tag line to exert its extraordinary power. It is also different from commercial brands in that it doesn't function primarily to drive business back to its point of origin, the way that, for example, Procter & Gamble hopes its skillful deployment of the Tide brand will drive up laundry detergent sales.

Of course, many companies and other organizations hope that their use of generosity *will* have the effect of raising their profile or their profit.

But that's an indirect effect.

While the generosity brand is different from any organizational brand, it can often comfortably coexist with these other brands. Nonprofit organizations such as the Kellogg Foundation and the March of Dimes have been known as generous for a long time. What's new is the way that many for-profit businesses and even churches are ramping up their involvement in enterprises for the social good in the hope that it will weave generosity into their DNA in the public's mind.

These days, in fact, every organization needs to think about generosity in terms of co-branding: *How can we do good—and be seen as doing good?*

To answer this question for your organization, you need to understand the origin and peculiar nature of the generosity brand.

THE MAKING OF THE GENEROSITY BRAND

Generosity has always been around. Why has it become a brand unto itself only recently?

I don't think you can point to any single cause for the answer. Instead, all of the following causes (and more) have combined to create the branding of generosity:

The arrival of a cause-oriented generation

Members of Gen Y or the Millennial Generation (or whatever you choose to call today's young adults) are highly motivated by causes. According to a recent report, 75 percent of young people donated money to causes in 2012, and 63 percent volunteered time.[14]

Generosity comes naturally for this crowd. It's a part of who they are. I use frozen yogurt to describe the phenomenon: People from other generations may be like customers who go into a fro-yo store and casually select toppings to put on their yogurt. They start with a simple base of vanilla bean yogurt and add toppings all the way to the cash register. In other words, for them generosity can be an add-on to who they are and what they're doing with their lives. They may add on generosity to get a higher price point, or to add value, or to establish a better presence in the marketplace, or to lend a sweeter flavor to their name.

But for Millennials, there is no add-on, no essential division between their identity and their good works. They are not interested in the higher price point, the value-added equation, a better appearance, or any of the rest of it. Generosity is already totally blended in with who they are.

Too often, employers, pastors, and organizational leaders underappreciate the central place that generosity occupies for this generation. As Tyler Green—the Millennial grandson of the founder of Hobby Lobby and a generosity expert in his own right—reminded me, we fail to connect with these individuals because "we are not telling the right story. The generation before did the American dream: work hard to stack stuff up. The generation behind it wants to help people right now with their lives. They don't want to do *this* so they can go do *that* one day. They ask, 'Why can't I do it now?'"

I mentioned before that website Trend Watching labeled the current generation as *Generation G* for generosity. Here's what they said about all of the rest of us following the Millennials in totally blending generosity in to our organizations:

"Joining GENERATION G as a company or a brand is not really optional, it's a *fundamental requirement* if you want to stay relevant in societies that value generosity, sharing, and collaboration."

Joining obviously entails more than adding a social responsibility or sustainability department; it means adopting a generous mindset that permeates every interaction with your community, with your employees, with your customers, with, wait for it, your "stakeholders." It is nothing more or less than a *holistic approach to generosity and business.*[15]

"JOINING GENERATION G AS A COMPANY OR A BRAND IS NOT REALLY OPTIONAL, IT'S A FUNDAMENTAL REQUIREMENT."

The worldwide love affair with sustainability

Organizations everywhere are talking about how to become economically, environmentally, and socially sustainable.

From factories cleaning up their wastewater discharge, to multinationals supporting education in the developing countries where they hire, to agricultural corporations investing in organic growing processes, organizations are trying to pursue their mission over the long term while minimizing the damage they might do in the world. This helps to bring generosity's concerns right into the inner workings of organizations.

In a recent sustainability report, Tyson Foods highlighted the following achievements:[16]

+ 18 million pounds of protein donated to hunger relief agencies since 2010
+ 11 percent reduction in water consumption at Tyson plants since 2004

- nine new products introduced in the last year that met updated USDA school standards
- reduced greenhouse gas emissions and waste sent to landfills
- investment in ultra-light equipment to increase transportation efficiency

Companies everywhere are pursuing similar measures because they know they are going to receive scrutiny for sustainability—and it's not only good for others, it's also in their own best interests.

The leveling effect of technological advances

No longer is it just the foundations and not-for-profit organizations with large media budgets that can gain attention for their work. Through communications technology, even those engaged in the smallest of efforts to do some social good can now find help and expose their work to whomever might be interested. Do you want to start an organization to help orphans in a village in Africa? Fine; go ahead and create a Facebook page to start building a group of followers. Don't know how accomplish something? Well, Google "How do I _____?" and in minutes you'll have enough information to warrant a master's degree on the topic. Too impatient to apply for foundation funding? Get your seed money through Kickstarter or one of the other crowdfunding platforms. A movement may be only one viral tweet or YouTube video or Instagram post away. It doesn't take a big bank account to buy an iPhone and get rolling.

Technology can…

… show a need from anywhere on the globe in real time, right now.

…allow me to access just about any information with no delay.

…let me network with others and find the help I need.

…provide immediate feedback from the field.

…unleash new funding opportunities.

…permit even a small organization to create world-class videos to highlight their work.

… connect a team spread around the globe for better synergy and effectiveness.

…offer off-the-shelf solutions to capture and organize data and track giving.

All this and more is in reach of any generous group, thanks to technological advances.

The involvement of celebrities

For a long time now, since well before Michael Jordan raked in obscene sums to hawk Nike shoes, celebrities have been leveraging their visibility to advertise products.

Sometimes an upstart has ridden celebrity popularity to almost instant success: think of GoDaddy with the likes of Danica Patrick and Jean-Claude Van Damme.

What's new is the extent to which the generosity brand recruits people to do the same thing. Instead of promoting hamburgers or luxury cars or smartphones, they're trying to get you interested in a program to feed the hungry, house the homeless, or heal the sick.

Angelina Jolie becomes the face of the United Nations' refugee agency. Bono speaks up for Amnesty International. Even Jimmy Buffett wants you to know about the Save the Manatee Club. It may be a symptom of the shallowness of our times, but recognizable figures bring generosity opportunities to the attention of millions.

The entrance of mega philanthropists

Of the thirty largest charitable foundations in the world, one-third didn't exist in 1980. The main reason for the recent surge is that some of the world's wealthiest people are getting into the giving game. The partnership of Bill Gates and Warren Buffett in the Gates Foundation is the best-known example of many.

The author of the book *Philanthrocapitalism* may go overboard with his subtitle: *How the Rich Can Save the World*. But surely the rich can do, and are doing, a lot.

Buffett and the Gateses have organized the Giving Pledge asking billionaires to pledge at least half of their wealth to charity. (Buffett has pledged 99 percent.) This effort not only ensures that vast resources will be directed toward charitable aims but also encourages some of the brightest business minds in the world to collaborate and creatively attack areas of profound need. Perhaps most importantly, though, it reveals a growing sense of both responsibility and empathy. Bill and Melinda Gates capture both these qualities in their personal pledge letter:

"Our animating principle is that all lives have equal value. Put another way, it means that we believe every child deserves the chance to grow up, to dream and do big things.

"We have been blessed with good fortune beyond our wildest expectations, and we are profoundly grateful. But just as these gifts are great, so we feel a great responsibility to use them well."[17]

The mega giving trend doesn't necessarily mean, however, that the rich give wisely or with the most impact.

In his book *Reinventing Philanthropy*, Eric Friedman points out that the rich tend to give to causes that make them feel good (for example, a new wing to a natural history museum in their city) rather than to causes that are profoundly important to a lot of people (for example, fighting childhood diseases in the developing world).[18] Nevertheless, the potential for good that their wealth embodies is immense.

THREE SHIFTS THAT LOCATE THE BRAND

With forces acting on them like the ones listed above, today's generosity is not your father's (or mother's) generosity. Advances in technology and the spread of information, in particular, are responsible for three trends that define what the generosity brand looks like today:

1. *The shift from indiscriminate giving to strategic giving*

It used to be that people would make contributions to an aggregator of gifts, such as their church or the United Way.

Now they're more likely to do research for themselves and give to a specific cause or group that matches their interest and that they believe will maximize the benefits of their gift. Large foundations and charities, similarly, are drilling down into the data and using new decision models to become more discriminating in their grant-making and gift-giving choices. Targeting has become the name of the game.

Daniel Harrell, senior minister at Colonial Church in the Twin Cities area, told me, "Churches are no longer the brokers of Christian giving. In the old days, you would give your money to the church at large and they would dispense it. Now the giver is in touch with the needs and causes. They have their passions and want their priorities addressed, so they want to manage the giving themselves."

2. *The shift from control over giving by institutions to control over giving by individuals*

My long-time friend Tom Addington—founder of Givington's, an online generosity shopping portal—says, "The consumer is sitting in the driver's seat, and the entire world of philanthropy and generosity is shifting to that reality. The consumer wants the choices."

No longer are institutions always in control of where the help goes; contributors are involved too. Some companies are letting customers vote on which causes they will direct monies to. The growth in donor-advised funds and other types of donor-directed giving is one of the strongest trends in philanthropy today.

3. *The shift from impersonal giving to personal giving*

Alan Gotthardt, managing director of TriniD Capital and author of *The Eternity Portfolio*, told me, "Most people don't give because of a strategy. They give because of a relationship."

He's right. All parts of the giving and philanthropic process are being pulled to a new north star: personalization.

Today the focus is shifting from fighting poverty (impersonal) to helping poor individuals (personal), from battling hunger or disease (impersonal) to helping specific men, women, and children who are afflicted (personal). The Susan G. Komen Foundation is just one group that has figured out how to take advantage of this renewed interest in personalization.

They don't make the pitch for you to shop pink or race for a cure simply to defeat breast cancer; they ask you to do it to support a friend, neighbor, or family member who has battled the disease. They want you to have a name and face in your head and on your heart.

Social media and forms of online communication have helped to enable the personalization of generosity. Tara Russell of Create Common Good explained to me, "Now there is immediate feedback and verification. I can touch, taste, feel *now*. I want to help this guy in India, and now I can know who he is and where his family's house is. It's all very personal."

Keeping it personal is naturally more motivating. And so the generosity brand keeps rolling.

GENEROSITY MARKETING

If you need proof that generosity has become a worldwide brand, look no further than marketing. Generosity has taken over marketing like water flooding a rice paddy.

What is known as "cause marketing"—a for-profit company using its clout to promote one or more compassionate causes around the world—used to be a curiosity. Now it's ubiquitous.

What's curious, in fact, is when a company *doesn't* engage in cause marketing.

Between 1990 and 2013, corporate spending on cause marketing in the United States grew from $120 million to $1.78 billion.[19] Aflac sells a plush duck to raise money for research and treatment of childhood cancers. Brooks Brothers clothiers collects used coats for homeless programs. Pizza Hut is working in early childhood literacy. Unlike corporate philanthropy, which is tax deductible, cause marketing is a business expense like any other kind of marketing. But it creates goodwill for the company at the same time it does good for worthy causes.

We could call this kind of marketing *generosity marketing*. It includes every strategy a company uses to promote itself while doing social good. Is it trying to do good? Yes. Is it trying to sell a service or product? Yes. Is it trying to build its corporate image? Yes. Is it trying to keep a competitive advantage? Yes.

Classically, marketing was about features and benefits. Now it's largely about values. My goal is to connect you to a higher purpose along with me, and then you will have greater loyalty to me. It's still marketing, but it's *generosity* marketing.

LOOK!

One way to evaluate generosity marketing is to consider where it shines the spotlight of attention. I would say that generosity marketing has three primary messages:[20]

Look at me!

Have you ever received a solicitation email from a nonprofit asking you to "Join us in X"? Have you ever seen corporate advertising that prominently conveys the message "We're helping out Y"? Has a church ever proudly let you know they're playing a role in the community by doing Z? There's no subtlety to the self-interest in these kinds of promotion. The emphasis is clearly on *me* or *us* before it's on the cause.

This doesn't mean the people involved aren't well meaning or aren't accomplishing good things. But it certainly lets you know that they are very much interested in putting themselves out there in the public eye under the banner of generosity. It might at least make you wonder about their sincerity.

Look at this!

The next strand of generosity marketing, instead of being obviously self-promoting, focuses on promoting a solution for a need. It might say that, if you want to keep poor families safer and reduce the destruction of forests, give $10 to The Global Alliance for Clean Cookstoves. Or it might ask you to help an organization defeat preventable blindness by giving to a trachoma eradication program. Whenever someone jumps on the bandwagon of the latest natural disaster, it's likely to be a case of "Look at this!"

"Look at this!" generosity marketing is more selfless than "Look at me!" marketing. And there's certainly nothing wrong with the pragmatism of solving a problem. But it's focused on process rather than people.

Look at them!

The final class of generosity marketing is done by organizations to "bring awareness" to the plight of those in need. This includes posting videos or messages on social media, mentioning a cause in company communications and advertising, sharing articles and interviews, celebrities and musicians addressing issues in public forums, and so on.

Its primary goal is not so much to point you to a solution as to bring to light and make real the situation demanding your attention. It tends to be very personal and focus on individuals affected by a problem. Unsurprisingly, then, "Look at them!" messaging relies heavily on the power of narrative to bring to life the folks who are in need. The idea is that we'll recognize our shared humanity with them and start to think about what we can do to make a difference for them.

All three of these types of generosity marketing have their advantages and disadvantages, both for the needy people and for the business doing the marketing. If there is a trend, it is toward "Look at them!" messaging. It's all very personal, and as I'll say in a future chapter, the recipient is the hero of the story.

THE BRAND FOOTPRINT

As big as commercial brands such as Coke, McDonalds, and Apple might seem, concept brands have the potential to get much bigger. To understand the generosity brand, you need to realize that the business of generosity is simply enormous. It is transforming one organization after another.

Entire industries and verticals are dedicated to generosity. B schools are creating courses about it, and major business journals devote articles to it every month. Generosity has a Godzilla-sized footprint.

And the brand is still growing. Generosity is not in a push phase; it's in a pull phase. And as the Millennial generation matures, its generosity mindset is undoubtedly going to spread and overtake all of society. Innovation, meanwhile, is rife, spawning diverse and energetic forms of generosity.

Think of what the business of generosity already encompasses (the following is a very partial listing):

+ Newly formed channels aggregate generosity, some with money (Givington's, Pure Charity), some with goods and services (*youshare.org*), and some with gifts-in-kind (Good360).

- Social media sites are bringing people together for conversations around generosity (Generous City, Giving Tuesday).
- Some organizations are using market-based models to address needs, including social venture capitalism (Acumen Fund), social impact investing (Ashoka), social entrepreneurship (Omidyar Network, Skoll Foundation), and microfinancing (Kiva Microfunds).
- Some companies identify themselves as social enterprise or socially conscious brands (Full Circle Exchange, Raven + Lily, Whole Foods).
- Established corporations are rediscovering sustainability practices, such as the way Nestlé is adopting good water practices.
- Some missionaries and church organizations are using the business-as-mission model to enable them to get into resistant nations for spiritual work.
- Websites are enabling everyday folks to become their own small-scale philanthropists (Jolkona, *DonorsChoose.org*).
- In addition to the diversity of generosity approaches, we also see how powerful generosity really is when we realize how much it affects our own identity.

We know that people can identify with commercial brands. Someone might tell us, "I drink Pepsi. I watch *The Voice* on TV. I always buy the new version of *Grand Theft Auto* when it comes out. I'm a United Methodist. I do my work on a MacBook." This helps us peg him in our minds.

The same kind of brand transference happens with generosity. What we care about, what we give to, what we volunteer for defines, at least in part, who we are and what we care about.

A buddy of mine said, "Our cause alignment and giving is part of our personal brand. This is the same as a Fortune 500 company translating their brand." Someone might say, "I support charity:water" or "I care about human trafficking. If you get that, then you get me better."

Our cause alignment becomes a part of our personal branding. In this way generosity reaches inside our own lives at the same time it transforms the structures of the society we live in.

THE SELFISHNESS OF GENEROSITY

Clearly, being generous is cool. Today everyone (or so it seems) wants to do good for others. And if you're on the receiving end of this generosity, it can be an amazing thing.

But the hipness of the generosity brand aside, it brings some problems with it. For two, there are inauthenticity and judgmentalism.

How generous are you, really?

In the business of generosity, organizations almost always have a double purpose. Yes, the fact that Coca-Cola temporarily suspended its advertising helped it devote more money to Typhoon Haiyan relief. But that very suspension of advertising gained highly valuable publicity for the company— and that was no doubt a part of the plan when it was hatched in Atlanta. I don't mean to pick on Coca-Cola. Good for them for helping storm survivors. The fact is, the same dynamic plays out all the time when companies try to do well by doing good. Generosity marketing is always both an end in itself (the generosity part) and a means to an end (the marketing part).

But for-profit businesses are not the only entities with a double purpose in their generosity. Nonprofit organizations that depend on donors also hope to gain attention for themselves through what they do, thus growing their ability to do more good works in the future. And even if NFPs as organizations seek a low profile, those working inside them and their donors likely get a return in the form of approval from others or at least a personal sense of meaning and satisfaction.

In short, generosity is rarely 100 percent altruistic. There's almost always an admixture of self-interest. And it's very hard to root that self-interest out (if that would even be desirable).

We *can* say, though, that blatant attempts at self-aggrandizement through trying to co-opt the generosity brand have a way of backfiring. Millennials, especially, have their poser antennae out. They will not give you many chances to sound disingenuous or inauthentic—one strike and you're out. The authors of an article on generosity marketing wrote,

> While these campaigns do provide much-needed support to worthy causes, they are intended as much to increase company visibility and improve employee morale as to create social impact. Tobacco giant Philip Morris, for example, spent $75 million on its charitable contributions in 1999 and then launched a $100 million advertising campaign to publicize them. Not surprisingly, there are genuine doubts about whether such approaches actually work or just breed public cynicism about company motives.[21]

That's one way of being inauthentic. Here's another: Jeff Shinabarger says, "The greatest concern, as businesses become more generous, is that they are telling stories that are not true. People promise things that they are not doing. Or come up with shallow, short-sighted solutions."

Some organizations are out-and-out frauds. Every major disaster brings out scammers, such as the charity group that raised $700,000 for a quilt honoring 9/11 survivors and never produced the quilt.[22]

On the list of America's worst charities are many that have given less than 1 percent of their funds away in aid.[23] Hundreds of suicides in India have been linked to microfinancing companies that were unscrupulous about recovering debts.[24]

Even the best-intentioned generosity organizations can go wrong. Books such as *Toxic Charity, When Helping Hurts, The Spiritual Danger of Doing Good*, and *The World Is Not Ours to Save* warn of hubris and carelessness in generosity works.

So we're left with some hard questions about what's real and what's viable in generosity:

Do you have a house divided when the profit motive commingles with an impulse to help others?

In other words, might mixing business and generosity lead to being distracted from the business and amateurish at the generosity?

If generosity marketing campaigns are designed to trigger obligation, guilt, or compulsion, are they appealing to people's worst nature instead of their best? Is it even possible to be motivated by compassion and justice to do generosity marketing, or are shame, fear, and guilt the only real muscles that move the consumers?

Will competition lead marketers to oversensationalize social problems or to overstate what an organization is doing to defeat those problems?

As generosity marketing grows, will it cause so much noise that people will begin to tune it out?

Are some people so eager to adopt the generosity brand that they will throw money and resources at problems they don't really understand and maybe exacerbate the problems in the long run?

Are we reaching a point where the explosion of foundations, nonprofits, and initiatives is becoming reduplicative and wasteful?

Has generosity fatigue perhaps already set in?

Will cynicism eventually grow until it fatally tarnishes the generosity brand?

Will organizations quietly pull out of the generosity business when it no longer serves as a competitive differentiator?

Don't you care?

These days, we're wearing our causes on our sleeves. And on our T-shirts. And on our wristbands. And on our Facebook pages and our Twitter feeds. And inked into our skin. And stuck on our car bumpers.

We slap stickers on our shirts announcing that we voted or gave blood, and we bombard our friends with email solicitations to sponsor our favorite charity run. Just mention human trafficking or poverty in Africa, and boy, let me tell you what I've been doing.

The notion of not letting your left hand know what your right hand is doing (Matthew 6:2-4) has gone the way of the dodo. What does that say about what's going on in our hearts as we practice generosity?

"AS GENEROSITY MARKETING GROWS, WILL IT CAUSE SO MUCH NOISE THAT PEOPLE WILL BEGIN TO TUNE IT OUT?"

It's not just a matter of pride. There is also a subtle, or often not so subtle, judgmentalism that comes out of our in-your-face identification with generosity.

Like certain other concept brands, generosity has "social weight." In other words, not only is the brand popular on its own merits, but in fact, many people actively exert pressure to try to get others to conform to the brand.

We've seen this script played out before. Back in the 1990s—the heyday of the "Made in the USA" branded concept—there was social pressure to buy American. Then in the 2000s, when "Going Green" first became a prominent branded concept, there was pressure to do the right thing for the environment by recycling, buying energy-saving light bulbs, and bringing your own bags to the grocery store.

Likewise today, when it comes to the generosity branded concept, there is social pressure to do good for others. This is positive if it means that more good is being done. But social weight can often lead to social ostracism.

If being generous is cool, not being generous is *not* cool.

Volunteering on your day off is cool. Skipping the volunteer construction day for Habitat for Humanity because you were too tired to get up early on a Saturday makes you a social pariah on a level with someone who kicks puppies.

Have you ever been to a party, finished a drink, and asked the host, "Do you recycle?" You can actually feel the withering stares and hear the angry thoughts of other partygoers if the answer is no. You may even detect an audible "How can you not recycle?"

Generosity is quickly attaining a similar social weight. Soon, if not already, you will hear others say, "How can you not give?" or "How can you not volunteer?"

What they will really be asking is, "How can you not care?"

The generosity brand is supposed to stand for people coming together to make a real difference. But when we let our corrupt human natures produce judgmentalism and falsehood, we have inverted the brand. And robbed it of its power to do good.

WHERE THE BRAND IS GOING

The generosity brand is not going away anytime soon. It is too blended into our thinking about supply chain and demand chain success. Thousands of young cause champions are born every day around the world, and if anything, they will amp up the power of the brand in the decades that lie ahead.

But even though the brand concept is here to stay, it will be filtered and tested like never before. The noise of the concept alone will mandate some movement. We will continue to see reconfigurations in the machinery that promotes this brand and seeks to fulfill its promise.

"THE GENEROSITY BRAND IS NOT GOING AWAY ANYTIME SOON."

FOR THOUGHT AND DISCUSSION

1. What do you think has most contributed to the creation of generosity as a brand?

2. Would you describe your personal and corporate generosity as strategic or indiscriminate? Why?

3. What is your personal experience with Millennials regarding generosity and cause?

4. How does the fact that generosity is its own brand impact business and ministry strategy?

5. What organizations do you know that do a great job at utilizing generosity and cause in their marketing appropriately and seem to be authentically integrated in their approach?

6. On the flip side, who is doing it poorly?

7. Of the three messages seen in generosity marketing—
   "Look at me!" "Look at this!" "Look at them!"—which
   is the most prevalent? Which is the most effective?

8. How important is story in today's culture, and who
   does the best job of that in your experience?

9. How does an organization avoid a self-serving
   appearance in its marketing and storytelling?

10. What do you think will be the next stage in the
    evolution of cause marketing?

CHAPTER 3

THE GENEROSITY ECONOMY

*Generosity flows from givers to receivers,
and then around again.*

GENEROSITY IS MUCH more than just kind wishes toward those in need. It is purposeful action to improve human lives and the world. So generosity naturally assumes concrete forms to contain and direct the good intentions. That's why I refer to "the business of generosity"—there's organizational machinery in operation doing the work of generosity. And my business of generosity, your business of generosity, and every other business of generosity in the world today combine to form an entire economy of generosity.

This chapter is a brief study in the macroeconomics of generosity. What are the major forms and channels and iterations of generosity organizations? How are they changing? Why are some thriving while others aren't?

We're going to cut through the complexity. Let's begin with some backstory to American generosity.

GENEROSITY IN OUR DNA

Every nation of the world has its own tradition of generosity. Generosity in the United States of America has a quality all its own, full of vigor and can-do optimism and colored by America's religious history and capitalistic bent.[25]

The early European settlers of North America saw immediately that they would have to rely upon each other's help to make it in the New World. Puritan leader John Winthrop viewed his Massachusetts Bay colony not only as "city upon a hill," but also as a "model of Christian charity."[26]

Benjamin Franklin, who seems to have been the first to do almost everything in colonial America, was also a leader in civic responsibility. Among other things, he organized the nation's first volunteer fire company and established the first subscription library.

Modern social sector bloggers and members of giving circles may think they're doing something original, but they are really standing in the tradition of the Junto Club that Franklin founded while still a young man. Every month he would gather a small group of businessmen at a Philadelphia tavern to lift their ale cups and talk about ways to improve themselves and benefit the community.

In the nineteenth century, a wave of social reform movements swept the country, focusing on what today we would call "causes"—abolition, temperance, women's voting rights, and many more.

Look at someone like Clara Barton, founder of the American Red Cross, or Jane Addams, co-founder of Hull House to assist poor immigrants, and you realize that social entrepreneurs existed long before Muhammad Yunus started talking about them.

When America's growing wealth created her first millionaires, these men began to practice philanthropy in a form we recognize today. Of course, Americans had always been giving away money, especially in the form of offerings to churches. But when a titan of commerce like Alexander Graham Bell, for example, began using his wealth to find solutions for deaf people, it was a sign that the great era of foundations and corporate giving had begun. In 1889, steel magnate Andrew Carnegie wrote "The Gospel of Wealth," in which he encouraged his fellow rich folks to use their wealth to improve society (foreshadow of the Giving Pledge). Carnegie and Standard Oil founder John D. Rockefeller established modern American philanthropy, with many more to follow in their footsteps.

After World War II, when America entered a period of greater affluence and influence in the world, the number of foundations and nonprofits of all kinds began to skyrocket.

No longer was it just the wealthy who engaged closely in generosity; average folks began to see that they could be philanthropists too. The advent of the information economy in the late twentieth century put tools for innovation within reach of all. American generosity today is more participatory and diverse than ever.

HOW GENEROSITY MOVES

Think of it this way: Generosity is like a substance that is meant to fill the empty spaces created by the needs in the world. This "substance" comes from a source, flows along a channel of some kind, and hopefully arrives at its intended destination. The business of generosity encompasses everything that is required to get generosity to flow to where it's needed.

As we've said, generosity is more than just money. It's also gifts-in-kind, volunteerism, and so on. But money is a big part of it, and money serves as a more convenient metric than anything else. By following the money, we see at once that there are givers and there are receivers making up the generosity economy.

As I mentioned in Chapter 1, in the United States financial giving by individuals and organizations totals approximately $300 billion per year, which is equal to 2 percent of the gross domestic product. Americans volunteered their time in an amount roughly equal to $171 billion.

Most of the money and volunteer efforts that Americans give passes through a vast array of religious congregations (more than 300,000) and other not-for-profit organizations (around 1 million) on the way to the people who need the generosity. If you're like most people, you may occasionally hand over some cash to a panhandler on the street (the shortest possible flow of generosity), but you direct most of your charitable giving to NFPs such as your local rescue mission, the Sierra Club, the American Heart Association, or whatever other group is doing work you want to get behind. These organizations have expertise in getting generosity where it ultimately needs to go.

Givers and receivers. It can all seem so neat and orderly, hardened into accepted patterns. Actually, the situation is anything but orderly and unchanging. The business of generosity, in fact, is in a ferment. Today, generosity is springing up from new places, and flowing in new ways, more than it ever has.

CONVERGENCE, CREATIVITY, AND COLLISION

Many of the same forces that are driving change in the private sector economy are also switching things up in the social sector. Technological advances, interconnected communications, globalization, economic volatility, reduction in resources—these are some of the reasons why we're seeing so much innovation in the business of generosity.

The old verities are being called into question. Models are being torn down and rebuilt. The landscape is being rezoned. Laura Arrillaga-Andreesen titled her book on philanthropy *Giving 2.0*, and she's right—what we have today really is a distinct iteration of generosity in America. Some of it may be in beta form and may never survive its rollout, but the net effect of all the inventiveness, I can't help thinking, has got to be more of the "substance" of generosity filling the "gaps" created by needs in the world.

In a recent Giving USA report, researchers
tracked the money coming and going, and it looks
like this.[27]

MONEY FROM...

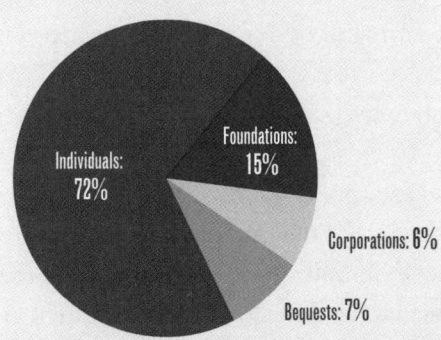

Individuals:
72%

Foundations:
15%

Corporations: 6%

Bequests: 7%

MONEY TO...

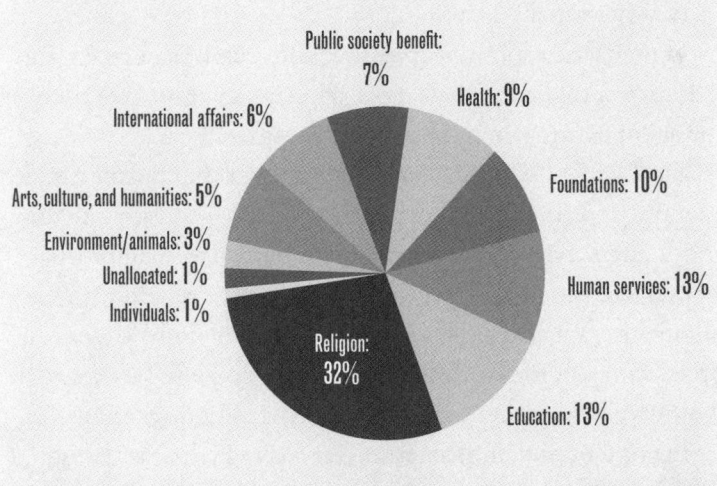

Public society benefit:
7%

Health: 9%

International affairs: 6%

Foundations: 10%

Arts, culture, and humanities: 5%

Environment/animals: 3%

Unallocated: 1%

Human services: 13%

Individuals: 1%

Religion:
32%

Education: 13%

There is high learning happening from channel to channel and from market segment to market segment. We are borrowing frameworks and tools from each other. The top-grading of best practices happens more quickly in today's environment.

The changes taking place in the business of generosity largely consist of a blurring of lines and a convergence and restructuring of both forms and practices. In the area of generosity, there aren't just houses and boats anymore; there are also houseboats of every make and description.

Businesses doing good

It used to be that for-profit businesses just focused on making money. It was assumed that was the way it was supposed to be. In fact, Milton Friedman famously said, "There is one and only one social responsibility of business—to use its resources and engage in activities designed to increase its profits."[28] But increasingly, businesses are trying to do good at the same time they are doing well.

Now let me slip in a caveat.

I know that a lot of people look down on business. As Tom Addington told me, "The act of giving is way more pure than the act of earning, in most people's minds."

But I believe it's important to remember that businesses do a lot of good simply by doing business: they produce valuable goods and services for the world; they create wealth for their workers and shareholders; they have a way of providing a sense of purpose, spurring innovation, and breaking down barriers. So it's far from the truth that businesses do good *only* through their corporate giving programs or generosity marketing. But on the other hand, if businesses can leverage their cash and their knowledge capital to do good more directly, why not?

These two aims—doing good and profitability—are no longer mutually exclusive propositions, but rather two complementary corporate emphases. Mike Duke, former CEO of Wal-Mart, captures this relationship wonderfully, noting, "Being involved in social issues isn't counter to being profitable; it actually causes Wal-Mart to be a better business. We strive to run a better business, to be more profitable, and to serve customers better."[29] In short, doing good doesn't have to mean you lose profitability, and being profitable doesn't mean you aren't doing good.

Using the caterpillar-into-butterfly analogy, Whole Foods CEO John Mackey writes, "Corporations …can exist at a caterpillar level, where they strive only to maximize their own profits, extracting resources from nature and from human beings to do so. Or they can reinvent themselves as agents of creation and collaboration, magnificent entities capable of cross-pollinating human potentials in ways that nothing else can, creating multiple kinds of values for everyone they touch."[30]

The Coca-Cola Company gives around 1 percent of its operating income annually to improve the living standards of people around the world. According to their reports, they partner with governments and private organizations involved primarily in the four areas of water stewardship, healthy and active lifestyles, recycling, and education. In 2011, the Coca-Cola Foundation invested more than $76 million in 257 community organizations around the world.[31]

The examples could go on. Drug maker Eli Lilly has a patient assistance program reducing the cost of prescription medications for uninsured and underinsured patients.

Through its Network for Teaching Entrepreneurship, MasterCard releases its finance-savvy employees to give business lectures as volunteers in schools. According to the *Chronicle of Philanthropy*, the U.S. company that gave away the most money in 2012 was Wells Fargo, banking on the social sector in the amount of $315 million.[32]

Meanwhile, businesses are finding new ways to help. Some for-profit corporations are starting their own nonprofit foundations or not-for-profit arms. They are working for good with specific causes or in specific locations. In the process, they are looking more like small, nimble private companies.

When my daughter Katelyn buys a pair of TOMS shoes at the Masons boutique in Fayetteville, where we live, the good folks at TOMS donate a pair of their canvas slip-ons in one of more than fifty countries. TOMS is the best-known practitioner of the *buy one, give one*, or BOGO, model of generosity, but it's far from the only one. Buy a pair of eyeglasses from Warby Parker and they'll give another pair of glasses, or comparable funding, to one of their nonprofit partners focused on improving eyesight.

If you buy a comforter from the Company Store, the retailer will donate another comforter to a homeless child living in a shelter somewhere in the United States.

Then there is what I call "channeled capitalism." This is a model within the world of online shopping in which someone buys something and creates a margin or surplus, which is then directed to a needy person or project. For example, if you place the iGive button on your browser, a percentage of your purchase prices at online retailers can go to a cause you support. Pure Charity tailors a shop-and-earn program to put "charity rewards" into your own Giving Fund. Givington's will direct charity through your purchases.

And eBay Giving Works enables shoppers to donate to nonprofits and sellers to direct a portion of their sales to nonprofits. Want to know how much they've given away? Check out the real-time counter at their website (the number reaches into the hundreds of millions of dollars!).

As businesspeople are trying to be more organically generous, whole new forms are being created to contain business-charity hybrids.

B (for benefit) corporations are for-profit entities that consider society and the environment in addition to profit in their decision making. L3Cs (low-profit limited liability companies) are another kind of entity that facilitate investments in socially beneficial for-profit ventures.

Foundations taking over ground from government

Governments are the largest generosity providers in the world, even though they're often not even included in discussions about generosity. Take this one example alone: New York City, through its taxing powers, provides $25 billion annually for education in city schools. No nonprofit could match that kind of giving. Foreign aid, domestic entitlements—these and many more kinds of giving by governments small and large around the world are utterly immense.

One can also argue, however, that they are immensely wasteful, even if they are necessary. And from a problem-solving perspective, the answer they seem to offer is always "More of the same."

The New Deal, the Great Society, and all the other government efforts to improve lives have failed to eliminate many problems and arguably have created some others.

It's not surprising, then, that some wealthy individuals are making noises about taking the reins back to raising up those who have needs. Foundations are taking initiative by forming partnerships and coming up with strategies to finally defeat intractable problems.

Perhaps in a more coordinated approach, government can take its rightful place as a larger, though less nimble and certainly not all-capable, partner in addressing important needs, along with giving entities, nonprofit activists, and faith-based groups.

Nonprofits making profit

Every year, I participate in dozens of nonprofit board meetings or conversations with board members about their nonprofit work. And I can't think of a single one of these conversations in recent years where the subject of alternative revenue streams did not come up. No nonprofit, it seems, wants to be fully dependent on donor giving. Every nonprofit would like to find some other way to bring in cash to fund their efforts and to grow. Many are experimenting with, or at least considering, ways to earn a profit.

Just as for-profit businesses are looking more like nonprofits, it's also true that nonprofits are in many cases looking more like businesses. This is often called the *earned income model*. Fees for goods and services make up around 45 percent of total nonprofit sector revenue.[33]

In certain areas of nonprofit work, earned income through sales and fees plays a huge role. These areas include health care, education, and the arts. Also, larger nonprofits are more likely to earn income than smaller ones.

But more and more, other types of nonprofits are experimenting with alternative streams of income. I've worked with poverty missions that sell crafts from the Third World,

---

"REVENUE-GENERATING INITIATIVES ARE BEING LAUNCHED OR CONSIDERED IN VIRTUALLY EVERY NONPROFIT DOMAIN, FROM HUMAN SERVICES TO HOUSING TO THE ENVIRONMENT."

---

churches that supplement their offerings with rents from store space, and many other nonprofits benefiting from the earned income model. They may never make huge sums from it like the $2.4 billion brought in annually by Goodwill stores. But if it might enable them to grow and do more good, they're willing to try it.

The earned income model has been around for a long time—the first Girl Scout cookie was sold in 1917, the first UNICEF card was marketed in 1949. But it's getting interest today like never before.

As the authors of a *Harvard Business Review* article on the subject say, "Revenue-generating initiatives are being launched or considered in virtually every nonprofit domain, from human services to housing to the environment."[34]

Why are more nonprofit leaders turning to profits to support their mission? I've heard a few reasons.

- It's more appealing than constantly making an ask.
- Reupping every year with a zero balance can be tiring.
- It can be a differentiator from other, similarly missioned nonprofits.
- It can raise visibility and expand volunteer contacts.
- The money comes without strings attached.
- It can help predictability in funding.
- Managers of nonprofits want to be viewed as entrepreneurs.
- Board members, with a background in business, encourage it.

Establishing alternate streams of income is not without its challenges and limitations. But for many nonprofits, it's another way to accomplish their mission.

In the case of churches, acting like a business may raise special theological questions. Are they getting away from being who they're meant to be? Daniel Harrell says, "Some churches have gone whole hog in adopting full-on business practices without filtering out the business values that don't specifically apply to the faith community." But done right, profit making can accrue even to the benefit of the service of God.

Fundraiser Dan Pallotta, in his book *Uncharitable*, argues that the entire nonprofit sector needs to become like its for-profit counterpart in even more fundamental ways than just earning income.[35] He says that society's nonprofit ethic acts as a strict regulatory mechanism on the natural economic law. It creates an economic apartheid that denies the nonprofit sector critical tools and permissions that the for-profit sector is allowed to use without restraint (for example, no risk-reward incentives, counterproductive limits on compensation, and moral objections to the use of donated dollars for anything other than program expenditures).

These double standards place the nonprofit sector at an extreme disadvantage to the for-profit sector on every level.

While the for-profit sector is permitted to use all the tools of capitalism to advance the sale of consumer goods, the nonprofit sector is prohibited from using any of them to fight hunger or disease. Capitalism is blamed for creating the inequities in our society, but charity is prohibited from using the tools of capitalism to rectify them.

The answer, then, would be to move even more radically in the direction of nonprofits acting like for-profit entities.

Most churches would say that their primary purpose is to bring glory to God. But more and more churches are strategically reorganizing to engage in material service to man alongside the spiritual worship of God. They are exhibiting a renewed sense of responsibility to care for "the least of these."[36]

This is much more than hosting a Thanksgiving dinner for the homeless in the church basement. Some churches are starting the equivalent of endowments and legacy-giving chairs.

They may look more like a university setting or a small business or even a foundation than the traditional image of a local church.

This kind of thing is happening even more frequently in new church starts founded by younger leaders. There is a recovery of energy to see the gospel make a sustainable difference in the renewal of a community and in service of those in need. As Martin Luther King Jr. said, "The Christian gospel is a two-way road. On the one hand, it seeks to change the souls of men, and thereby unite them with God; on the other hand, it seeks to change the environmental conditions of men so the soul will have a chance after it is changed."

My own church has spun off an organization called Samaritan Community Center. Trying in a broad-based way to help the poor of northwest Arkansas, the center provides meals for the hungry, sets up mental health counseling, pays for doctor and dentist visits, provides children with backpacks stocked with school supplies, sells used clothing and furniture at bargain prices, and just recently started a garden/farm.

Although the center has become independent, it is still housed in the 19,000-square-foot building donated by the church, is still run by church members, and still offers its practical services in the name of Jesus.

To help organizations of all types think more broadly about what they can be accomplishing, I use the acronym MBL.

MULTIPLE BOTTOM LINE

A single numerical figure at the bottom of the balance sheet, regardless of its size, can no longer measure success. Our whole world is quickly migrating toward an expectation that all efforts return something beyond a single bottom line.

For some time, people have talked about the double bottom line—aiming for profits and something else. In 1994 John Elkington coined the phrase *triple bottom line*. His three bottom lines were *people, planet,* and *profits*. In 2006, Andrew Savitz published a book called *The Triple Bottom Line* and continued the dialogue, emphasizing the social, environmental, and financial performance metrics for success.

I like these three categories, but I think people of faith can do Savitz one better. Savitz doesn't split the spiritual good apart from the social good, and I think that's worth consideration. Therefore, I often describe four bottom lines that reflect money, environmental good, social good, and spiritual return.

Honestly, there are probably a number of possible bottom lines, but when I talk about "multiple bottom line," I'm thinking about these four categories:

+ *Profitability*—The obvious one. Are you making money?
+ *Environment*—Is your work replenishing the earth? Is it sustainable?
+ *Social good*—Are you providing jobs, opportunities, and social welfare for others?

Spiritual return—Is faith strengthened? Is the gospel being displayed as part of this work or intentionality?

If you're an organizational leader, multiple-bottom-line thinking is your protection against everything you don't want to become, and it is your power to effect the change you dream of. It is one of the greatest differentiators for all the right reasons and all the best results.

The Nehemiah Project, a Christian entrepreneurship ministry, outlines these four reasons for thinking about multiple bottom lines:[37]

1. MBL pushes you to think holistically about your business.
2. MBL looks to transform communities, not just display good citizenship as a public relations strategy.
3. MBL provides greater financial stability in the long term.
4. MBL produces more employee, shareholder, and customer satisfaction.

Multiple-bottom-line thinking puts your convictions to the test, but it can be good for business at the same time. Happier employees, shareholders, and customers usually produce a higher achieving and more stable company.

GENEROSITY'S BEST PRACTICES

It's good to know about the different forms and channels of generosity, whether traditional or newer, and the multiple benefits they can produce. But there's something even more important than the channels through which generosity flows, and that is *how* the flow happens within those forms. Just as businesses across industries share certain best practices that aid them in their striving for profits, so all sorts of diverse organizations that are effectively engaging in the work of

"IF YOU'RE AN
ORGANIZATIONAL LEADER,
MULTIPLE-BOTTOM-LINE
THINKING IS YOUR
PROTECTION AGAINST
EVERYTHING YOU DON'T WANT
TO BECOME, AND IT IS YOUR
POWER TO EFFECT
THE CHANGE YOU DREAM OF. "

sgenerosity tend to make some similar choices about how they do whatever it is they do.

Are there really similarities between a nonprofit hospital in Indiana, an evangelistic Christian ministry in Central America, and a legal team trying to root out the sex trade in Thailand? It turns out, there are. Generosity can thrive in just about any channel with the help of the following insights, guidelines, and collective right practices. Here are three universal best practices.

1. *Who's the hero?*

It's easy for big donors, celebrity spokespeople, or the leaders of businesses and nonprofits to want to attract the spotlight of attention toward themselves.

Look at me! Look at what we're doing! Many have made this mistake—and have been surprised to find their names stinking like yesterday's gym socks with the very people whose favor they sought.

Why?

Because the spotlight is pointing the wrong way.

The hero isn't the do-gooder; the hero is the one who is the object of the good that is being done. That should have always been the case, but sadly, it has not. Yet whatever tolerance for self-serving publicity may once have existed within the realm of generosity is fast evaporating. And this is true regardless of the type or size of the giving institution.

The spotlight has moved to a new spot on the stage, and it looks slimy to bring the attention back over to you after the entire cultural audience has shifted their gaze. The world is in rapt attention to the needs on the ground—the end point of those who are starving, marginalized, underutilized, and otherwise hurting.

Smart leaders shape the narrative of their organizations so that the focus isn't on an organization doing good but on the recipient of that good. If an organization tries to make itself the protagonist of the narrative, they will lose their generosity cred.

Of course, if yours is a company engaging in generosity marketing, or a nonprofit hoping to raise your profile, you want *some* attention for yourself. And here's where it gets dicey. You have to be careful, but as long as you never forget who the real hero is, you can get some indirect—and surprisingly powerful—attention for yourself.

Consider how AT&T handled the original TOMS Shoes commercial. At first the commercial is all about the shoe giveaway program. You don't see the AT&T logo or hear the company's name mentioned until twenty-eight seconds into the thirty-second commercial.[38]

Is using your leverage for someone else instead of yourself risky? It might be. Just maybe you'll be casting your bread on the water and will never see a crumb of it again. But usually it comes back. In today's business of generosity, what's really risky is insisting on making the most of your leverage for yourself.

2. *Organic tastes better.*

There's a second best practice any generosity organization can incorporate in its operating procedures. And that is making sure that the generosity fits comfortably with the organization's i.d.

Attempts to do good that are artificial, ill-fitting, or self-serving create a bad taste in the public's mouth. But if a generosity program is organic to the organization that is doing it, it will be more likely to survive and thrive. In other words, the generosity work needs to be core to the organization's mission, model, product lines, or service. Toy R Us works with Toys for Tots at Christmastime. 9Lives cat food supports cat shelters. Philadelphia Cream Cheese is partnering with nonprofits trying to end child hunger.

Now, the cause an organization supports doesn't necessarily have to be directly related to what it does. For example, a grocery chain can fund cancer research, or a tech company can get behind a local zoo. But the organization that's doing the good work had at least better become knowledgeable and committed about that work, merging with it.

Established companies that genuinely want to do good, as opposed to just looking good, can do it. But it may require some retooling of their ways. Robin Weekley Bruce of the Acton MBA says, "Backwards integration is the next iteration. Leaders are now having to make their values consistent throughout the company.

Coke says they are about happiness and sustainability, so the question is, are your employees and supply-chain relationships happy?" No longer is there a one-spot audit for generosity that focuses on the end game. A company's ability to be fully integrated into generosity takes a start-to-finish transformation, one that might take time and certainly will take a lot of effort. But it *is* possible. Even in a well-established, highly traditional company, some motivated intrapreneurs can spawn a socially conscious approach that will eventually overtake the whole institution.

3. *Force multiplier.*

In the military, a "force multiplier" is a strategy or technology that enables a fighting unit to have the same effect as a larger force would have without the "multiplier." This is what I picture when I think of the third best practice: collaboration.

Too often in the past, organizations engaged in generosity have been disconnected and competitive, even (or perhaps especially) when pursuing the same good.

This may have been helpful when it came to an organization's self-promotion, and it even may have opened up some spaces for innovation, but it also put limits on what could be accomplished.

Pamela Slim and Michele Woodward say, "Collaboration is the new competition." And thankfully, today more than ever, leaders in the business of generosity are building bridges between their silos. They're joining forces to create a greater impact on social problems. For example, the African Comprehensive HIV/AIDS Partnerships bring together the government of Botswana, the Gates Foundation, and pharmaceutical giant Merck to enhance Botswana's national response to AIDS.

Collaboration is a big idea to help solve many of the ills of our globe. When people in the business of generosity pool their expertise, ideas, and connections, and coordinate their efforts, it's the difference between addition and multiplication. Both the givers and the receivers win.

More than that, collaboration doesn't cost much. It's usually not hard to do. Just about any organization of any size, with any type of social focus, can do it.

An African proverb says, "If you want to go fast, go alone. If you want to go far, go with others."

Collaboration may be the most obvious no-brainer among generosity's best practices. We all want to go far.

RECEIVERS INTO GIVERS

Finally, a reminder.

In any healthy economy, there is mobility where people at the bottom are moving into the higher ranges. That's true in the economy of generosity as well. We need to remember that a particular flow of generosity is not meant to last perpetually. It's meant to resolve a problem.

C. S. Lewis said, 'The proper aim of giving is to put the recipient in a state where he no longer needs our gift."[39] I would take that further and say that the proper aim of generosity is to put the recipient in a state where he or she can begin contributing to others. Generosity begins to look less like a one-way channel and more like a circular flow.

"COLLABORATION MAY BE THE
MOST OBVIOUS NO-BRAINER
AMONG GENEROSITY'S BEST
PRACTICES. WE ALL WANT
TO GO FAR."

1. What countries do you think should be more involved in global generosity?

2. Why are the traditional roles of business, churches, and NFPs blurring in regard to generosity?

3. Are there appropriate roles that should be played by each channel (government, church, NFP, businesses)? Or does it not matter what they are doing as long as everyone is contributing?

4. What channel do you think has the greatest potential for greatest impact over the next ten years?

5. Do you think every organization is now expected to deliver a multiple bottom line (profitability, environment, social good, spiritual return)? Does this include NFPs and churches? Why or why not? How effective is your organization in regard to its multiple bottom lines?

6. What NFPs do you know that are successfully utilizing the earned income model to offset their donor solicitation? What makes this a good thing or bad thing, in your thinking?

7. What are the big dangers for churches that engage in more entrepreneurial efforts of product and service offerings?

8. What does it mean for a cause or generosity to be "organic"?

9. What makes collaboration difficult, and why don't we do it more?

10. What are some things your organization could do to extend its generosity reach?

CHAPTER 4

THE THREE COMPETENCIES OF GENEROSITY

Generosity flourishes when an organization does good, stays viable, and remains true to its mission.

I'M NOT AN airplane pilot, but I know a few pilots and have learned a few things about flight dynamics over the years. When you're piloting an aircraft in flight, you've got to have control over the roll, pitch, and yaw motions of the craft if you want to stay properly oriented. Lose control of your plane on any of the three axes, and you're going to send it out of equilibrium … and possibly straight to disaster.

Often it takes a few things held in tension to achieve the greatest success. Another example is in the world of design. Design experts have used a triad of desirability, feasibility, and viability to guide best outcome for over forty years. It is the nexus of those three where the best design sits, held in tension among the three. Or even in the world of football, NFL commissioner Roger Goodell was making the case that the formula for success for the NFL was balancing profitability, popularity, and safety. Those three must always be held in tension to achieve the greatest outcome.

Well, I have another triad to suggest. Generosity is grounded on three inter-connected competencies:

1. *Do good*—have a positive impact in one or more areas of social well-being.
2. *Stay viable*—bring in enough profits, donations, or other revenue to operate with year in and year out.
3. *Remain true*—know and stick closely to your mission.

Succeeding in any one of these three competencies is easy enough. Keeping on track with two of them simultaneously is harder, though most organizations manage it. But doing good *and* staying viable *and* remaining true over the long term— now, that's a tough piloting assignment for any organizational leader! But that's where real success is to be found in the generosity economy.

Generosity is grounded on three inter-connected competencies:

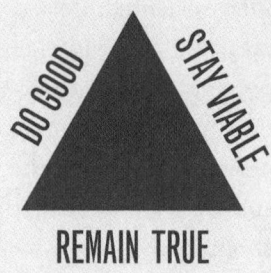

In fact, your organization *must* have stability in all three dimensions if you don't want it to crash and burn.

What do you find if an organization is failing in any one of the three competencies? A company intent on scooping up profits without regard to its impact on the community. Or a world-changing intention that disappears before it makes any difference. Or a good-hearted group of people who are drifting because they have no rudder to guide them.

Here's the story of one company that's doing generosity right in all three dimensions of competency.

THE CHICKEN AND THE EGG

Based in Northwest Arkansas, CCF Brands has the stated purpose of "improving lives by providing quality food products." A simple, clear mission, and one that the company sticks to. It sells eggs and other food items through such outlets as Wal-Mart, Target, and Albertson's, and in just over a decade of existence it has been successful in this to the tune of $300 million in annual sales and climbing. The profits are fueling the company's continued growth.

At the same time, this is a company that's doing much good, both internally and externally.

+ Environment: It's reducing waste and changing carton materials.
+ Food safety: It has created secure and sanitary facilities for handling food.
+ Animal welfare: It follows preferred animal husbandry practices for its hens.
+ Community service: It gives back to society through volunteerism, in-kind donations, and charitable contributions for local and national causes.

The company's second-generation chief executive officer Justin Whaley lives in the constant tension of succeeding in all three competencies simultaneously. It is not an easy assignment, but it is the kind of tension that produces a generous culture.

CCF is an example of an organization that is authentic in doing good. As we considered in the last chapter, it has organically integrated the generosity brand with its own branding, and it has done so since its beginning. Its employees feel good about working for this responsible-citizen company, and any customers who happen to research the company will be pleased to find out that they are buying more than just a carton of eggs with their money.

Doing good, staying viable, remaining true—CCF Brands is successfully navigating all three dimensions of the business of generosity.

DOING GOOD: NO LONGER OPTIONAL

Once upon a time, charities did good and businesses made money, and that was that. Oh, a company might have given away a small percentage of its cash through a corporate giving program, but that was optional and it was the extent of its involvement in doing good.

If the company made an occasional contribution, great. If not, no big deal.

Few, if any, are comfortable anymore with a view of business that is devoid of social responsibility. Today, it's all about combining social and economic success, both personally and corporately.

Steven Garber, a true gem of a guy and founder of The Washington Institute, introduced me to the good work being done by the food company Mars, for which Steven has served as a consultant. Here's a company that is striving for a thoroughly positive impact on the world. From working with a foundation to reduce obesity, to increasing yields of "orphan" crops that could provide good nutrition for millions of people in Africa, to moving toward a goal of using 100 percent fair-trade certified cocoa, to reducing water consumption, to fighting child labor in the nations where it has factories, Mars is pursuing specific goals to be a responsible global neighbor.[40] This kind of thinking and action is core to their DNA. They want to do good and be good and be known for good.

Doing good is quickly becoming (or may already be) a nonnegotiable aspect of doing business. Why?

+ *The best and brightest won't work without doing good.* As Millennials advance in the workforce, the importance of doing good will become paramount in attracting top talent to your organization. In fact, a 2012 Nielsen study found that 62 percent of respondents preferred to work for companies that give back. Of these socially conscious individuals, 63 percent were under the age of forty.[41]

+ *Consumers want more than a quality product; they want a socially positive one as well.* The same Nielsen study found that "two thirds of consumers around the world say they prefer to buy products and services from companies that implemented programs to give back to society ... nearly half say they are willing to pay extra for products and services from these companies."[42] According to another survey, "When quality and price are equal, the most important factor influencing brand choice is Purpose. Across the globe, the prominence of Purpose as a purchase trigger has risen 26% since 2008."[43]

Consumers are being retrained to expect more than just a functioning product and prompt service; they want social good as a standard add-on. Tyler Merrick of Project 7 told me, "We will return to companies and individuals who are quietly doing both sides—the giving of a service and product and doing good along the way."

+ *It's good for business on many levels, so not doing it doesn't make much sense.* Saving natural resources, making employees happy, building goodwill—things like these are all good for a business at the same time they are good for the world at large. Economists Michael Porter and Mark Kramer consequently argue that businesses need "policies and operating practices that enhance the competitiveness of a company while simultaneously advancing the economic and social conditions in the communities in which it operates."[44]

Your business ignores the social good at its peril. But let me issue a warning: As doing good has become a more integral part of business, it has also become more difficult. There is now greater accountability and higher expectations associated with generosity. In short, once you dip your toe in the water, you had better do it right. Too many people are doing the business of generosity well for you to do it poorly.

Some start-ups have made doing good the very purpose of their work (Sevenly). Others have tried to do their kind of business in a way that's more ethical than anyone in their line has done before (Burt's Bees). Some have been generous in giving away their profits (Ben & Jerry's). Some have addressed sustainability all the way back to raw materials and labor (Tegu). Whatever the best way may be for your business to enter the dimension of doing good, get moving on it.

Gabe Lyons, founder of Q Ideas, talks about the "common good," which is broader than personal advantage (what's good for an individual, family, or group) and is even bigger than the public interest (what's good for the majority in a society). It's about what's good for *everybody*. This is the mindset that is always looking for opportunities to be generous.

STAYING VIABLE: MONEY MAKES THE GENEROSITY WORLD GO 'ROUND

Doing good is no longer measured in one-time gifts and efforts. Today, doing good means addressing a problem, need, or injustice holistically, not just showing up with a big check or cutting a ribbon. It means being in for the long haul and staying invested until real change occurs. And that type of generosity depends on a sustainable organization. So staying financially viable is the second essential competency in the business of generosity.

Jim Collins says, "In a truly great company profits and cash flow become like blood and water to a healthy body: They are absolutely essential for life but they are not the very point of life."[45] A business that is pursuing multiple bottom lines had better remember that these still include the old-fashioned bottom line. It had better have the profits to fund its marketing causes and sustainability initiatives. Meanwhile, a do-gooder organization had better make sure it's attracting donations, sending out winning grant proposals, or earning income on the side. Achieving a mission is its point, but money is its lifeblood.

It's obvious: If you go belly up, you won't be helping people for long. Many once-marquee companies have vanished— Eastern Airlines, Arthur Andersen, Merry-Go-Round, RCA, and Burger Chef, to name a few. None of them gave any money away last year. Sure, a few people may have made enough money from these now-bankrupt businesses to start their own foundation or create a giving platform. But, overall, the loss of these companies means that the generosity curve has declined.

Lauren Bush Lauren, founder of FEED Projects, says, "Not every business is a bleeding heart. The businesses we partner with want to do good but also worry about the bottom line."[46]

Meanwhile, leaders at not-for-profits must always be thinking about how to keep the money flowing in. Sadly, many are not very good at it. In some charitable circles, it's even fashionable to have a kind of disdain for moneymaking.

On the other side of the coin, growing income means multiplying good. Shoe company Oliberté "strives to develop a thriving middle class in Africa by creating fair-wage, sustainable jobs in the heart of Ethiopia—and business is good."[47]

They're selling stylish shoes at a profit and in the process are making life better for poor people. Making money and doing good can naturally go together. It's no wonder that some of the most entrepreneurial parts of the world are also hotbeds of innovation and activity in generosity.

A friend of mine once said something that has stuck in my head: "Everything has overhead."[48] True. And that includes generosity. Because the business of generosity has overhead just like any other business, we need to bring in money somehow.

Now, doing good isn't just an impulse that should be directed at those in extreme need. Milton Friedman may have gone too far in trying to steer businesses away from charity, but he was right in saying that company leaders have a responsibility to employees, stockholders, investors, and suppliers.[49] A company helps these people through making a profit. At the same time, it keeps the organization going so the organization can keep doing good internally and externally.

STAYING TRUE: MISSION MATTERS

When I talk to leaders of generosity organizations about the need to do good and stay viable (competencies 1 and 2), it's usually an easy sell. They get it. They've already thought about these two aspects of their organizations. What they haven't thought about so much is the third competency: staying true to mission. Yet this competency is just as important as the other two.

Just about every organization was originally built around a missional core. Most still today have a precisely defined mission statement. For example, Nike's mission is "to bring inspiration and innovation to every athlete in the world." The nonprofit TED's mission is "to spread ideas." But even

"STAYING MISSIONAL,
ON THE OTHER HAND,
LEADS TO STABILITY AND
GROWTH. CAMPING OUT ON
YOUR MISSION MAKES IT
POSSIBLE FOR YOU
TO BUILD EXPERTISE,
CREATE A REPUTATION, AND
GENERALLY GET VERY GOOD
AT WHAT YOU DO."

organizations that have taken the time to draw up a cool mission statement can have a tendency to drift away from that mission in practice.

The result is an organization that feels to its public like it doesn't know who it is or what it's supposed to be doing. It might even feel inauthentic, like it's pandering to the masses instead of sticking to a passionate purpose. And these kinds of smoke and mirrors are always found out in the end.

Staying missional, on the other hand, leads to stability and growth. Camping out on your mission makes it possible for you to build expertise, create a reputation, and generally get very good at what you do.

Peter Greer, in his book titled *Mission Drift*, describes organizations that are Mission True and others that are Mission Untrue. He especially has in mind churches and parachurch organizations when he says,

> Without careful attention, faith-based organizations will inevitably drift from their founding mission. It's that simple. It will happen. Slowly, silently, and with little fanfare, organizations routinely drift from their original purpose, and most will never return to their original intent.[50]

In fact, any type of nonprofit, not just the faith motivated, can slide from Mission True to Mission Untrue.

What can cause your organization to drift from its mission? Many things. Here are just a few:

* *Adversity can throw you off balance.* If you have a bad quarter, or a big contract falls through, or an initiative fails, you may be tempted to either cut back on doing

good or jeopardize your financial viability. Either reaction threatens your identity as a generous organization.

+ *Success can make you arrogant or lazy.* Don't think it can happen to you? Check out Jim Collins's book *How the Mighty Fall* for an analysis of how even the best institutions can be tripped up by their very success.[51] Lose your motivation, lose your mission.

+ *Adapting too much because of customer wishes can gut your core mission.* All good strategy requires adaptability and occasional strategic pivoting, but that's different from being so swayed by market forces that you forget who you are. If you believe in your mission, don't trade partners in the middle of the dance every time someone winks or strolls your way.

Whatever the cause for drifting, the line at the bottom of the swim lane that can keep you headed in the right direction is knowing and sticking to your mission. If you haven't identified your values, mission, and vision, then do it.[52] Talk about your purpose often. Test whether you're being consistent with it from top to bottom in your organization.

COMPETENT ALL THE WAY AROUND

CCF Brands, the egg shipper, is contributing to all sorts of socially promising works (*doing good*). They're able to do that because they are turning a profit year after year (*staying viable*). And one key reason they are turning a profit is because they haven't forgotten who they are—a food supplier trying to improve lives (*remaining true*). This makes them a model for the business of generosity.

Whole Foods Market is another company that is fully active in all three dimensions. They define their mission as being "a dynamic leader in the quality food business." In their

"Declaration of Interdependence," they say, "We create wealth through profits and growth" alongside such social goods as practicing environmental stewardship and supporting local and global communities.[53]

In his book *Conscious Capitalism,* Whole Foods CEO John Mackey argues from his own experience for a fusion of profit growth and social value creation for all people.[54]

Besides CCF and Whole Foods, many other organizations are succeeding in the three competencies of generosity as well. Is yours?

If you're making money and staying missional but not doing good … you're not in the business of generosity at all.

If you're staying missional and doing good but not making money … you're on the way to extinction.

If you're doing good and making money but not staying missional … you may become irrelevant before you even know it.

Every business needs to make sure it's succeeding in its core competencies. In the same way, your organization needs to periodically revisit the three dimensions where your business of generosity operates and make sure you're doing it right. That's what makes you soar.

"IF YOU'RE STAYING
MISSIONAL AND DOING
GOOD BUT NOT MAKING
MONEY... YOU'RE ON THE
WAY TO EXTINCTION."

---

1. What makes it so difficult to achieve all three competencies—do good, stay viable, remain true to your mission?

2. Would you say that most companies find one of the three competencies naturally harder than the others?

3. How do you know if an organization is truly doing good?

4. When and where have you seen generosity to be good for business?

5. Do you agree or disagree that every organization is now expected to do good, regardless of its mission, structure, and offerings?

6. What companies do you know that have collapsed and left a city or entire region worse off because of their lack of sustainable viability? Conversely, what companies are contributing generosity the most to your community and region?

7. Has the higher degree of accountability in the business of generosity been a positive influence? Or has it led some to hesitate for fear of failure?

8. Which piece of the competency triangle do you think is most critical for your organization to focus on right now? Why?

9. What can push us off center with our mission?

10. How do the parts of the triangle—doing good, staying viable, remaining true to your mission—work together and work against each other?

CHAPTER 5

GENEROSITY'S ROI

Generosity is transformational for both the receivers and the givers.

UNTIL JUST A few years ago, Malti was a teenage girl living on the streets of Dehradun, northeast India, in the foothills of the Himalayas.[55] Her parents had separated from the family, and Malti had taken over the responsibility of caring for herself and her three younger siblings. She was making a pittance as a beggar and sometime "ragpicker," or street trash collector. She was uneducated, ragged, dirty, smelly, and ill, showing signs of the beatings and abuse that are all too common for defenseless street children.

Then one day she met a local woman named Shaila, who was one of the leaders of a program called Street Smart, providing food, education, and vocational training for street children in the area.[56] Malti immediately accepted the invitation to join this program, and gradually she began to heal in the loving environment it provided. Her horrendous background had somehow failed to rob her of her dream to make a better life for herself and her brothers and sister. Irrepressible and upbeat, she was always the first in line for everything Street Smart was offering.

After two years of receiving the help that Street Smart provided, Malti was ready for the next step in her transformation.

She took a job as a stitcher with a handmade textiles company called JOYN, whose tagline is "joining artisans to markets, bringing joy to communities."[57] Started by an American named Melody (Mel) Murray, this company's primary purpose is providing work for the poor of Dehradun—in other words, people just like Malti. But make no mistake, JOYN is a quality business. The company's distinctive block-printed handbags and other fabric accessories are getting noticed around the world, featured in such outlets as Refinery29 and TOMS Marketplace.

Malti has flourished at JOYN, in her turn making the work experience better for her co-workers with her smile and gift for laughter. With her earnings at JOYN, she has bought a plot of land where she intends to build a home for herself and her siblings. She has longer-range plans to start a grocery store.

The Malti of today is almost unrecognizable as the grown-up version of the dirty and impoverished street child she used to be.

I learned about Malti's story because Mel Murray and her husband, Dave, are friends of mine from Northwest Arkansas.

I have seen firsthand their determination, motivated by Jesus' example of compassion, to move overseas and create sustainable solutions for the very poor. (Dave founded a high-end guitar-making company in Dehradun at the same time Mel started JOYN.)[58] I've heard about the challenge it has been for them and their two little boys to adjust to life among the poor of India, and I have witnessed the joy they are experiencing within the close-knit community they have found with people like Shaila and Malti.

Dave and Mel have been transformed by the business of generosity, just as have their formerly impoverished employees. To me, their story is a stand-out example of the truth that the business of generosity should result in a return on investment. A transformation takes place. Something changes for the better. And just as there are many currencies of generosity, as we saw in Chapter 1, so there are many kinds of return on investments in generosity.

GOOD FOR YOU

It might seem obvious to say that generosity is supposed to do somebody some good. But surprisingly, in the business of generosity, the results are sometimes overlooked because the emphasis is placed on the process instead of the outcome. We can be more involved in the *busyness* of generosity than the *business* of generosity. We can be satisfied with *feeling good* about our generosity efforts and never evaluate how much we are actually doing good. But in the end, generosity is really supposed to be about *doing good*.

Every time they go to work in the morning, Mel and Dave Murray can see the transformation that has taken place in the lives of their guitar-making or fabric-weaving employees. Likewise, when a publishing conglomerate has diverted some of its cash to a literacy program as its chosen marketing cause, or when a multinational shipping company has used some of its logistics savvy to help speed relief to natural disaster victims, then they'd better expect that more people are learning how to read or the newly homeless have a tent over their heads.

It's about getting something done. Foundations should expect that the nonprofits they disburse money to will accomplish their stated goals.

Churches should want the employment counseling office or addiction rehab center or domestic abuse halfway home they have set up to result in people who are working gainfully or free of drugs or safe from a beating. Individual donors will want to know that they have made the right choices for the limited resources they are able to give away to help people.

And it's not even just *people* who are the beneficiaries of generosity. Puppy mill opponents are trying to make life better for the dog population. The Nature Conservancy is protecting ecologically valuable parcels of land because it's good for the species living there. Different recipients, but the same goal of achievement.

Books with titles like *Strategic Giving, Money Well Spent,* and *Give Smart* reflect a resurgent desire, not just to be generous, but to be generous *effectively*. Throughout the generosity channel, the players should be looking for results.

Now, I know that some results of generosity are harder to measure than others. If your organization is sponsoring construction of a neonatal unit in Haiti, you know when you've reached your goal—the unit is operating and preemies are getting treated.

Child sponsorship organizations can enumerate the kids in their programs, and medical research nonprofits can list the reports they've published. But if your mission is "to use music to bring people together," how will you prove you've done it? If you're a group of physicians treating people in a war zone, are you going to ask them to fill out a satisfaction survey? When Charity Navigator announced that it would begin scoring charities on results, they got as many catcalls as cheers.[59]

I also know that generosity's ROI doesn't always have to look "big." Not every generosity business is going to have a goal as ambitious as eradicating malaria worldwide (a goal of the Gates Foundation). A gesture of goodwill that gives hope, the patient turning around a life that has gone astray, any targeted outcome that is local or limited yet richly achieved—these kinds of "small" outcomes are just as important as the "big" ones if you happen to be in need of them. Every one is worthy of a celebration. Every one should give satisfaction to the generosity workers involved.

And then there's the timing reality. In some cases a result doesn't appear until well down the road.

It might take a whole generation to measure the full impact of what you're doing if you're involved in education or environmental reclamation or any number of other good works that require patience. As the saying goes, "You don't measure a tree until it has fallen." Premature measuring of the transformation that generosity is producing won't show the true picture, but that doesn't mean the transformation isn't happening.

All these things are true. But big or small, easy to measure or hard to measure, quick to mature or slow to mature, generosity is still supposed to create genuine transformation of some kind.

For people living under the biblical worldview, the concept of stewardship informs our results orientation. The money and other resources in our control are not ultimately ours but God's, so we are even more motivated to make sure we are deploying them for the social good as strategically as we can. Those with the gift of giving, or those who do philanthropy for a job, if they see themselves as stewards, certainly need to measure the impact of their gift. Those who direct the giving or charity must defend their ROI and treat it as a straightforward investment.

We want to be able to give a favorable accounting to the original Giver who has "microfinanced" every one of us from His unlimited stores. We're all there somewhere in the parable of the talents.

When I talk about the change potential of generosity, I ask people to think about how others have been generous to them through the years. Try it yourself: Family members, teachers, neighbors, and other caring adults helped you learn what you needed to know when you were growing up, didn't they? Perhaps a coach came through with a word of praise just when your self-confidence had been withering. Perhaps a Big Brother or Big Sister turned you aside from the route to disaster with a well-timed display of tough love. Perhaps an anonymous benefactor supplied money to help you with your education or a business start-up. And all this is continuing to pay dividends in your community, your nation, and beyond as you are a productive and generous member of the human race.

You've been the recipient of generosity that made a difference. Your generosity toward others should be funneled in the direction of making a difference too.

Generosity does good for others. But that's not the surprising part.

GOOD FOR ME

In Chapter 2, I addressed the ways that selfishness can get mixed up with generosity, leading to conflicts and dilemmas and quite possibly resulting in more harm than good. There's no question that we can easily become phony or self-righteous if we're not approaching generosity from a place of integrity. An "It's about them; it's not about me" mentality makes all the difference between pretense and productivity.

But even though doing good for others, rather than feeling good ourselves, should be our principal objective, there's nothing wrong with feeling good or getting certain other benefits from our generosity as a secondary effect. In fact, it's normal and proper for someone on the giving side of the generosity transaction to receive an ROI for himself. So much advantage comes out of generosity that you can't restrict it to the intended recipient—you've got to expect some blowback of goodness for yourself!

Generosity has a transforming effect for both individuals and organizations that give.

Individuals

Our own generosity changes us in so many ways. To start with, it changes how we view ourselves. We may approach generosity in the first place with an arrogant, superior attitude. (How many missionaries and philanthropists have been— often rightly—accused of that?) Kevin McCollum, executive director of Lightbearers, described the situation this way: "There is a high table and a low table. Folks with the money sit at the high table, and those asking for the funds sit at the low table. This can create bad psyches on both sides, arrogance at the high table and despair at the low one." Fortunately, our pride has a way of getting burned away when we spend time in the crucible of generosity. Working with others who are broken, we recognize our own brokenness. We finally realize that generosity isn't about getting a lift over others but rather about lifting others up.

In this process, generosity changes what we prize. Whether you chalk it up to survival of the fittest or our sinful nature, we all have a tendency toward self-preservation and self-absorption. Among other things, this means we get tightfisted.

But as we engage in generosity works, our valuation of money inverts as we see some of the luxuries that once enticed us as so much foolish fantasy compared to the all-too-real needs others have. We appreciate better what we've got. We shed our entitlement mentality. We foreswear our allegiance to the idol Money. Our clenched fists turn into open hands.

Peter Greer of HOPE International says, "When you capture enough of the American dream, you sit back and ask the deeper questions of life, like what brings meaning and fulfillment? God made us to be givers, and it creates joy."

Generosity also changes how we see others. We see them as our fellow humans, who though hurting or in need, are not inferior to us. In fact, there is a common thread among all people, whether we are giving or receiving generosity—and that is our humanity. And humanity has always implied, and will always imply, imperfection and fragility. We all need help; we can't make it on our own completely. Generosity bridges our isolation and brings us into community, just as Dave and Mel have found a new, loving community in northeast India. We all sit at one table.

The changes for individuals are particularly dramatic when we don't just give away money but rather give of ourselves, getting personally involved in the lives of the people we are trying to serve. We volunteer to help others, but in the process we wind up helping ourselves. In her book *Giving 2.0*, philanthropy strategist Laura Arrillaga-Andreesen cites two studies showing that people who volunteer are healthier and happier than those who don't.[60] Our problems are put in perspective and we're more fulfilled through working with other people.

For some individuals, generosity can in fact be downright redemptive. An extraordinary leader and friend comes to mind. Catherine Rohr started a program called Prison Entrepreneurship in the Texas corrections system, teaching inmates basic business skills.[61] In five years, five hundred convicts graduated from the program, sixty of whom started their own businesses when they got out. The recidivism rate among the program graduates was one-quarter that of the general prison population. These were lives being turned around.

But then came the time when Catherine herself found some kind of redemption through generosity.

She committed some moral transgressions, and when the news of this came out, it resulted in her getting barred from the Texas correctional system. The scandal made the news and was profoundly humiliating to Catherine. In speaking to groups about her work before then, she would sometimes try to spark empathy for prisoners by rhetorically asking, "What would it be like if you were known for the worst thing you ever did in your life?" With the scandal, now she felt outed and branded by her own worst failure. What was left for her?

She started over again. She went to New York and founded a new organization called Defy Ventures, a year-long program that teaches ex-cons how to start their own businesses. She understands her clients better now, and they accept her better too. Defy Ventures is enabling her to defy the power of her past mistakes to determine her future.

Organizations

Just like individuals, organizations also go through generosity-induced transformation. They receive an ROI on their giving too.

In the case of nonprofits, generosity is their *raison d'être*. Generosity is, or ought to be, the dominant gene in their DNA strand. Being involved with the people they are helping keeps them hewing closely to their mission.

Similarly, in the special case of those nonprofits called churches, generosity keeps them well rounded and well grounded. Like the two beams of the cross, they don't operate just in the vertical dimension of worship and obedience to God but also in the horizontal dimension of loving and serving people. My pastor friend Jim Hall pointed out to me that the Christian church's founder Himself created these two axes to focus the church's attention (Matthew 22:37-39 NIV).

This is what matters:

+ *First Commandment:* "Love the Lord your God with all your heart and with all your soul and with all your mind."
+ *Second Commandment:* "Love your neighbor as yourself."

Jesus modeled the pattern by living and ministering among the poor. (In fact, He was one of them.)

After He left the scene, deacons were quickly appointed alongside the apostles to oversee a feeding program for poor widows. The apostle Paul later collected funds among the Gentile churches of the Mediterranean for famine victims in Judea—an early example of a "cause." And it was in this context that he said, "Whoever sows generously will also reap generously" (2 Corinthians 9:6 NIV), as clear an affirmation as you could wish for the blowback of goodness in the business of generosity.

The Christian church from the very beginning has been involved in practical service. To the extent that it is recovering this vision in the new era of generosity, while holding on to the Jesus orientation that makes its contribution to the needs of the world unique, the church is becoming more like what it has always been meant to be. Service to others is in fact an imperative for all churches, large and small, liturgical and casual, wealthy and poor, urban and rural, contemporary and traditional. And with the clamor for generosity that's getting noisier by the day in our society, it's no wonder that growing churches today are ones that are serving with passion, innovation, and effectiveness in Jesus' name.

Like churches and other nonprofits, for-profit companies also see some measure of transformation coming out of their generosity efforts. If their corporate giving programs are seen in the community, they make good neighbors. If their cause marketing really makes sense as marketing, they earn favorable publicity, attract top talent, and score new sales. If their sustainability measures are successful, they conserve resources and set themselves up for long-term profitability. If they are fully integrated and organic in generosity, then they will become a good place to work.

But beyond all that, getting involved in social work alongside moneymaking has a way of changing a company's culture. The work seems to matter more, motivating employees. The attitude of service spreads to internal customers as well as external ones. The hard edge of business gets worn away and its impersonal nature becomes humanized.

Every organization ought to hold within its conscience the weight of using its footprint, leverage, and brand to bring redemption and transformation. That might feel like a stretch to some, but it really isn't. It's simply the way of the business of generosity.

RAISING YOUR GI

When I say generosity is transformational and redemptive, I mean it in the biggest sense possible. It changes the world. It changes the future.

As much as we want to learn how to do good for others and to make sure that our particular business of generosity is effective, there's a sense in which the larger results are out of our hands. And that's a good thing. Without intending to sound too mystical, I think that's the way it's supposed to be.

This generation didn't start generosity, and we won't end it. In fact, we never know where the ripple of our generosity will extend. We never know whose life will be changed by our work, or whose life will be changed by theirs, or by theirs … and so on.

This is more than just "pay it forward." Generosity is a heuristical practice: As a generosity community, we do something, see what happens, and figure out what to do next at that point. Again and again and again. Along the way, amazing opportunities appear, either for us or for someone else to take advantage of. This is why I say we shouldn't try to overcontrol our business of generosity. We have to make space for generosity's power of self-replication to operate.

So by all means keep learning about the business of generosity and your own place in it. But don't let your lack of knowledge or your doubts hold you back from actually going about the business of generosity. Remember, generosity comes from the heart. So if a love for others lives inside you, you're qualified! Make a start. Get together with people who have a similar desire. Try. Learn. Have fun. Fail and try again. Get better as you go.

Make it your business to keep raising your Generosity Index.

"WE NEVER KNOW
WHOSE LIFE WILL BE
CHANGED BY OUR WORK,
OR WHOSE LIFE WILL
BE CHANGED
BY THEIRS, OR BY
THEIRS ... AND SO ON. "

1. Do you think generosity should have a ROI? Do you measure the effectiveness of your generosity? If so, how?

2. Name five acts of generosity by others that have shaped your life.

3. How have you have been changed by your own attempts at generosity?

4. Can you remember a time when your genero-sity had as big of an impact on you as it did on the receiver of your help?

5. What is the most dramatically impactful generosity effort you have ever been involved in?

6. What has been your experience with churches regarding their engagement with the first and second commandments?

7. How do you measure transformation?

8. If transformation doesn't happen, does that mean the generosity wasn't worth it? How do you measure what is "worth" being generous toward?

9. After reading this book, what are your next steps? How will you change your generosity efforts?

10. What are some big and small generosity goals in your life? What are you doing to achieve them?

GENEROSITY QUICK GUIDE FOR BUSINESSES

1. Make money consistently. It is hard to be generous when your success is random and sporadic. You don't necessarily have to be profitable every quarter to be a generosity player, but if you are consistently losing money, your energy and capability for generosity will inevitably lessen. Maintain your enterprise viability, which will in turn put you in position for sustained generosity. Remember, it takes all three competencies: doing good, staying viable, and remaining true to your mission. Include all three in your corporate debate and scorecard.

2. Make sure your internal customers (employees) feel your generosity before you applaud what you are doing around the world. Know your internal customer sat (satisfaction) scores. Too often these individuals are overlooked in the generosity equation. Outwardly focused generosity is wonderful—you should give to causes and needs in your community and around the world. But the folks making that generosity possible must also feel appreciated and valued. Be generous to them with your time and with your resources. The biblical idea of expanding concentric circles of impact (Acts 1:8) is a great guide in this regard: Judea = your own employees; Samaria = your local community, backyard, and neighborhood; uttermost parts of the world = uttermost parts of the world.

3.   Be honest and meaningful in your marketing. Refuse to get into a race to out-sensationalize your competitor. Don't just ask what the customer wants to buy. Make sure you don't sell your soul to the market. Hold your center. Is your story true? Is it meaningful? And if at all possible, be humble in telling it. (I am not sure marketing can be humble, but at least give it a shot!)

4.   Collaborate! Collaborate! Collaborate! Don't try to function as the entire generosity supply chain. Find partners, and collaborate to achieve an even greater impact. Find other organizations that you can champion and that you can depend upon. Where would Wal-Mart be today without their unique partnership with P&G in the 1990s? It usually takes a collaborative talent pool to achieve something really big.

5.   Structure and staff for strategic generosity. Larger companies must be sure to staff and structure for strategic outputs that make a material difference. This is fundamentally different than just doing the same ole thing year after year, writing the same checks to the same people and showing up at the same benefits. This approach naturally builds in generosity leadership and accountability. Small and mid-sized companies can explore getting creative with a dedicated employee or a consulting engagement to help achieve similar results.

Organization: *CCF Brands, Rogers, Arkansas*
Individual: *Scott Page, vice president of people and culture*

Scott's previous job was being a shepherd and builder of people as a pastor in a local church. Scott's current job is being a shepherd and builder of people tied to an industry-leading private company called CCF Brands (mentioned in Chapter 4). His job is to make sure the right people are in the right seat on the bus, they are being developed effectively, and the company is actually achieving its robust mission to be a MBL company known for excelling in all three areas of generosity competency. As a senior leader in the company reporting to the CEO, he is expected to bring both ideation and accountability, when needed, with regard to all things people and culture.

6. Be organic and transparent. The more pure and organic you can be the better. This is especially important with regard to Millennials, who comprised 50 percent of the global workforce at the end of 2013. What does it mean to be organic? If your core business is drinks and beverages (like Coke, Pepsi, Anheuser-Busch), then help out with issues related to water and thirst. If your expertise is in transportation (like UPS, J.B. Hunt, or FedEx), then make sure you are part of the supply chain solution steering help from point A to point B. If you are a food producer or distributor (like Tyson, Kraft, or General Mills), then tie your company to reversing poverty by battling food insecurity. If you are in real estate, then ... You fill in the blank. The same applies to every sector and industry. This is exactly the concept Robin Weekley Bruce defined as "backward integration." Coke says they are about happiness and sustainability. So that claim has to now be applied everywhere—all the time, not just in the Super Bowl ad campaign. Are your employees and supply chain relationships happy?

Organization: *Project 7, San Clemente, California*
Individual: *Tyler Merrick*

In 2008, Tyler Merrick launched Project 7 with the goal of giving business profits to worldwide need. Along with Blake Mycoskie and others, Merrick was one of the first members of Gen X or Y to create a company with cause and generosity baked into its business offering and its reason for existence. With the taglines "Products for Good" and "Change the Score," Project 7 sells everyday goods such as bottled water and chewing gum and donates a percentage of profits to seven areas of worldwide need (hunger, homelessness, etc.). The products are in retailers such as Caribou Coffee and Forever 21, and in the past six years they have planted 3.4 million trees and have provided 1.2 million meals, 150,000 days of schooling in Africa, 32,000 days of shelter to individuals in need, 20,000 days of counseling to children of war, 30,000 malaria treatments, and a year of clean water to more than 40,000 people.

7.   **Empower the Millennials to lead** (or if you're a millennial ... lead). Millennials are motivated and wired differently than other generations, especially when it comes to the issues of cause and generosity. It is a fundamental part of their makeup, and they have an incredible energy to make things happen. Take advantage of this drive to move the needle in your company. That might feel risky, and it might not turn out like it would if you were leading the charge, but that just might be a good thing. Give them the keys to the bus and empower them to be catalysts for change.

8.   **Pull in all the employees.** For years, generosity decisions were made by a small handful of folks. They picked the cause, picked the amount, and that's how the check was cut. I know it adds a layer of complexity, but consider making your generosity a company-wide and company-culture issue. There is no one right way to do this. Learn the causes that inspire your employees. Create situations that encourage and applaud generosity. Help employees give more and make a greater impact. The more people who are involved, the more your company can experience the transformational power of generosity.

Organization: Northstar Partnering Group and Field
Agent, Fayetteville, Arkansas
Individuals: Henry Ho and Rick West

*We often think of individual generosity and corporate generosity as
two entirely separate channels. Individuals give to and volunteer for their
preferred causes, and companies write checks and donate goods to the
favorite causes of owners and senior leaders.*

*As the business of generosity evolves, the artificial walls between these
channels are breaking down and organizations are working with their
employees to expand their generosity impact.*

*Henry Ho and Rick West have done an incredible job of encouraging
this type of company-wide, participatory generosity at Northstar
Partnering Group and Field Agent. Among other things, they allow each
team member an extra week of annual vacation to be used for a mission-
focused trip. These trips can be for international or domestic efforts. They
can be for inner-city ministries or suburban church plants. The employee
picks the trip, and the organization gives him or her the time.*

*The company also provides matching funds to support individual
giving to 501(c)(3) groups, which allows employees to make a greater
impact for their favorite causes. Any unused matching funds are then
distributed to partner ministries each year.*

*Generous individuals are great. Generous companies are great.
It's even better when they can combine their generous efforts for the
maximum possible good.*

GENEROSITY
QUICK GUIDE FOR
NOT-FOR-PROFITS

1. Don't be only self-consuming. I often say, "Most NFPs never met an asset they didn't want." Cash? Food? An old used car that hardly runs? They will take it! The truth is, most NFPs are almost always short on funding. Few are flush with cash and capability on a regular, ongoing basis. Because of this, they can inadvertently become self-consuming organizations, primarily focused on keeping themselves afloat. After all, it's not easy to be generous and outwardly focused when you aren't sure how you will pay the light bill. To keep this tendency in check, build in intentional reflection and accountability to ensure you are remaining true to your mission.

2. Empower the Millennials to lead. As mentioned earlier, Millennials are motivated and wired differently than other generations, especially when it comes to the issues of cause and generosity. It is a fundamental part of their makeup, and they have an incredible energy to make things happen. Take advantage of this drive to move the needle in your organization. Use their numbers as well. Millennials are flooding the world of NFPs and impact companies. Welcome them and empower them to succeed.

3. Collaborate! Collaborate! Collaborate! Don't try to function as the entire generosity supply chain. Find partners and collaborate to achieve an even greater impact. Find other organizations that you can champion and that you can depend upon.

4. Modernize your generosity metrics for success and effectiveness. Whether you agree with Dan Pallotta or not (see Chapter 3), his point of view is challenging much of the traditional way we have thought about and measured success for the NFP community. Since most NFPs are in the transformation business, you must figure out your model and how you are going to measure that transformation and gauge success. This is no easy assignment, but don't shrink back from it. Wrestle through the mud to figure it out and then get all the stakeholders aligned and on board. And be sure to flip the pages as new best practices emerge.

5. Glean from the innovators. Keep your finger on the pulse of trends and innovations in whatever your area of impact may be. Know who is tackling similar work and how they are doing it. Stay nimble and be open to better, more effective ways to accomplish your mission. Too often, NFPs waste time, money, and energy going backward and sideways because they think no one is doing what they are doing. You rarely have to reinvent the wheel. Keep your radar sweeping for others doing similar things and better things in order to learn on their dime. Otherwise, you might have to spend your whole dime and day to learn something easily learned from another.

Organization: *Praxis Labs, New York City*
Individual: *Dave Blanchard*

Dave Blanchard and Josh Kwan founded Praxis Labs with the conviction that the future of our world depends in part on the ventures the next generation creates. Praxis annually selects a dozen nonprofit and a dozen for-profit start-ups to participate in a year-long accelerator program where a group of experienced mentors offer insight and practical advice to would-be entrepreneurs. There's a $100,000 prize for the winner of the competition, but the real prize is the relationships with mentors and funders and the exposure in new insights and strategy. Mentors regularly connect Praxis participants with old friends and business partners and acquaintances who might be a few laps ahead of their younger understudy.

6.   **Balance the appetite of local and global.** I've noticed an interesting trend in recent years—organizations that are global want to go local and those that are local want to go global. There is nothing wrong with a desire to expand your reach or localize your impact. Both can be healthy impulses, but both can also push your model into a different risk zone and disrupt your success formula. In many cases, these desires may be best met by partnering with someone else.

7. **Settle your revenue model and get some traction.**
Figure out a healthy, ongoing blend of donor solutions and revenue-driving initiatives. And figure out your optimal structure for effectiveness and impact. There isn't a one-size-fits-all template for every organization. Some organizations need multiple structures; some need just one. Some need to lean entirely on donor revenue, and others need a higher percentage of non-donor revenue. Whatever mix you land on, don't chisel it in stone. Take a look at your model and mix every two or three years to see if a pivot is order.

Generosity Snapshot: Structuring for Generosity

Organization: *Westaway Law, New York City*
Individual: *Kyle Westaway*

Attorneys usually get a bad rap for generosity, but Kyle Westaway never fit the attorney mold. He's an attorney, but he's also a writer for publications such as the The Wall Street Journal and a social entrepreneur who co-founded Biographe Blanks, which provides employment for former sex workers. As a fresh mind on new models and structures, Kyle counsels social entrepreneurs on the best ways to structure their organizations, helping them think outside the box to consider ideas such as filing as a low-profit company or flexible-purpose corporation in order to maximize the business and philanthropic goals. Infrastructure, after all, goes a long way in turning good intentions into sustainable generosity.

8. Never forget: people give to vision, not need.
I have heard people say this for years, and I still seem to always forget. At the core of what most NFPs do lies the basic function of asking others to share their resources with you. To do this well, and do it over time, you need to craft a story that is both compelling and future oriented. Relying on pleas of urgency "I need your help," "The situation is dire," and "We need your help NOW" is the least successful tool for fund raising. Get a vision that moves people, not just to put out a fire, but to get involved with their whole being ... more than once.

Generosity Snapshot: Partnering for Generosity

Organization: Redeemer City to City, New York City
Individual: John Hutchinson

John Hutchinson leads the ministry of Redeemer City to City, originally founded by Redeemer Presbyterian Church in Manhattan (pastored by Tim Keller). Years ago, Redeemer decided that its vision of churches in the city and for the city should extend beyond their city. Today, City to City trains thousands of aspiring church leaders each year, and over the last decade the Redeemer network has planted more than three hundred churches in forty-five cities around the globe. But whether Amsterdam, Cape Town, Tokyo, or Moscow, their model for helping foster city renewal around the globe depends on many people being a part of the supply chain. Partners and friends have been crucial to their impact.

GENEROSITY
QUICK GUIDE FOR
INDIVIDUALS

1. **Don't outsource the intelligence or decision making.** Own the heart and mind of your generosity. It is your stewardship responsibility, not someone else's. Sure, get some legal and accounting tips along the way, but stay in the driver's seat of engagement. Keep your mind and heart out of neutral.

2. **Don't let wealth change you for the bad.** Don't live by the high- and low-table mentality, as my buddy Kevin McCollum explained in Chapter 5. His business model allows him to be on both sides of the table—giver and receiver—which has helped him shape his mindset of generosity. "Those who have the money should work very hard to set the emotional tone and relational tone," he says. "They need to have incredible humility and joy in the chance to give." And so should we.

3. **Set up the right structures.** When I recently read the helpful book *Giving 2.0* by Laura Arrillaga-Andreesen, I was reminded that having the right structure is crucial to your generosity agenda. In a quick summary on pages 93–95, she highlights nine vehicles for individual giving. If you don't have the book, get it.

4. **Practice random acts of generosity (RAG).** It is important to not be overly programmed or formulaic with your generosity. Yes, think it through and make a plan. And yes, be smart and strategic. But stay sensitive and responsive to the needs and opportunities that you may encounter each day.

5. Spend some money to advance your learning.
Network and attend gatherings to stay sharp with best practices, and establish a peer group to process your specific situation. Utilize the web to find learning venues. There are a number of these across both domestic and international lines. Find one that fits your style and personality, but also one that can challenge you with new thinking.

Generosity Snapshot: Learning about Generosity

Organization: *The Gathering, Tyler, Texas*
Individual: *Fred Smith*

Do you ever feel that the areas of giving and helping can be really noisy and crowded? It often seems that everywhere you turn there is a new cause, a new foundation, or a new celebrity trumpeting the most urgent need. Many may feel the impulse to engage but simply don't know how and where to cut through the noise and start.

Enter Fred Smith and the international association he leads: The Gathering.

The Gathering exists to provide information and perspective for individuals, families, and foundations committed to giving in the Kingdom of God. They don't solicit funds for any particular ministry. They don't pressure you to give or to give more. They simply provide a setting at their annual conference for like-minded people to gather and share ideas and learning connected to the concept of giving. People leave making their own giving decisions, but as part of a network.

---

6. Pull your whole family into your giving thinking and plan. Set up a giving mechanism and get your family involved, even the young kids. Just like in an organization, the more people you involve, the greater the chance for transformation to take place at a family level. And few parents will ever recognize a higher ROI than building a generous heart into their children.

Generosity Snapshot: Intergenerational Generosity

Organization: *Kalos Group, LLC*
Individual: *Greg Spencer*

In 2005, Greg and Laurel Spencer set up a mechanism to intentionally encourage and cultivate a spirit of generosity in their children. They created a flexible, structured fund and enlisted their kids (late teens and early twenties at the start) as "fund managers." Their hope was to not only help those in need, but also, while doing so, involve their children in the process and teach them to think long term with impact investing.

Although the implicit desire is to spend the fund down, it has smartly replenished itself each year, pushing the project's sunset further down the road. Every year, typically around Thanksgiving, the family holds a meeting to review the rolling five-year plan and make decisions about immediate giving channels. Each child is designated an amount to manage, and the intention is to transfer more and more of the fund management to the children. The fund's resources go to international and domestic causes. The gifts are small and large, and all carry the expectation of good stewardship and full reporting back to the family. This practice has become part of the spiritual identity of the Spencer family.

7. Collaborate! Collaborate! Collaborate!

Embedded in the concept of stewardship is the concept of leverage. And one way to leverage a donation or investment is to link your effort with someone else. Learning how to partner is not automatic and often requires some extra work from the individual. We are usually more comfortable controlling all the variables, but in doing so we lessen our potential impact or the ROI for our generosity.

8. Figure out how to effectively and authentically live in a world of tensions.

My friend Bill Townsend talks about this all the time. I have to learn to live with and in tension: pay your bills, save for your kid's college, be smart with your investments, and still be generous, sacrificial, and other-person oriented. Ruthlessly trust in God, but work hard at the same time. And always remember, stuff and significance don't always ride in the same car.

9. If you have a positive financial event, get aggressive with your generosity.

From time to time, you may be fortunate enough to get a bonus or a big raise or to sell a company. At these intersections in your life, strengthen your generosity muscle. Too often we simply pay a penance and consume the rest. Instead, use the unusual influx of cash to boost your generosity.

Organization: *Married couple*
Individuals: *Bill and Mary*

What do you do when your annual bonus arrives in the mail or is deposited in your bank account? Most of us probably throw a bit in savings, maybe pad the retirement account, or add a little extra in the vacation section of our family budget. Not Bill and Mary.

I was fortunate enough to meet this couple some years ago as I was helping to gather resources for an individual in need.

Bill and Mary heard about the need and approached me, immediately giving upward of $10,000 to the cause. Why? Well, Bill and Mary were working professionals who received bonuses on an annual basis. Years ago, they established a practice that dictated that they didn't consume those bonuses. Every dollar goes to causes, every time. They built it into their lives, and no matter what, no matter how big or small the bonus, they give it all away.

GENEROSITY
QUICK GUIDE FOR
CHURCHES

1. Empower the Millennials in your congregation to lead this effort. This, of course, assumes that your church has some Millennials. If that is in fact true, recruit them to lead this effort. If the Millennials are not leading this effort, you are missing some serious mind and muscle. Empower the Millennials among you and give them the keys to the bus … really!

2. Collaborate! Collaborate! Collaborate! Don't try to function as the entire generosity supply chain. Don't try to invent and house everything in your backyard. If someone else is operating a hunger relief program, make sure that you can't help them before you start your own and double-spend and double-build in the community. Find other organizations that you can champion and that you can depend upon. Get exposed to what is happening in your community and who is doing it. And this includes other denominations of churches and "secular" agencies. These are often some of the best places for collaboration. Too often, the church community suffers from lack of exposure.

3. Preach generosity as a way of life. Make generosity a way of life, not simply something that is owed to the church. Don't just give money—visit, pray for, and promote your partners. Encourage parishioners to give to more than the church.

4. Embrace both the first and second commandments (Matthew 22:37-39) in your vision, spending, staffing, and structures. Make generosity a part of the central gospel message and mission of your church. Set up a framework and formula for your giving. Decide how much of your tithes, offerings, and special gifts will be spent for buildings, staff, and your church versus how much is going to be directed outward to others. Set it up early before the numbers get too big, the structures and staff load get too large, and it becomes almost impossible to course-correct.

Generosity Snapshot: Intentional Generosity

Organization: *Briarwood Presbyterian Church, Birmingham, Alabama*
Individual: *Frank Barker*

Over fifty years ago, when Frank Barker helped launch Briarwood Presbyterian, he did so with a unique financial imperative built into the church's DNA. Coming up with the "50/50 Rule," Barker and those who joined him in Briarwood's early years agreed to direct fifty cents of every dollar that came into the church back out again. Fifty cents of every dollar would go to things like missions, community outreach, and benevolence. This meant, of course, that only fifty cents would stay in the church for traditional budget items, such as staff and building projects. To this day, the church has never wavered. In comfortable years and in lean years, fifty cents of every dollar has gone outward to the business of generosity.

5. Get innovative when you have windfalls or transition events in the church. It is common for churches to go through life cycles where they need to relocate or reboot their future. It is also common for established churches to find themselves with more assets than they typically possess. Too often, though, we don't know how to redeploy those assets for maximum influence and impact. Jump out of the box with your thinking and embrace new possibilities to leverage those resources, especially at life-cycle intersections.

Generosity Snapshot: Leveraging for Generosity

Organization: *Colonial Church, Edina, Minnesota*
Individual: *Daniel Harrell*

Up in the Twin Cities area is an old-school-looking church with a new-school idea of how to spur generosity in ways far beyond the offering plate. Colonial Church, pastored by Daniel Harrell, runs the Innové Project, which provides $250,000 in seed money to organizations with viable plans to "change the world." The 2013 applicants included Exodus Lending, which helps stressed borrowers move to financial stability, and Beyond Limits, which enables independent living for individuals with disability. Applicants submit an idea with the goals of receiving practical help and winning seed money. In this way, Colonial Church becomes an encouragement to generosity rather than simply a recipient of generosity. When the church had a chance to convert unused land and leverage those assets, they picked an innovative pay-it-forward approach that would bring a MBL for years to come.

6. Staff a dedicated leader. Find someone with the right wiring and passion to lead your generosity efforts, and recruit him or her. This person can increase the overall intelligence and exposure of your generosity efforts. He or she can customize generosity for your church and community, working methodically with the congregation.

Organization: *Fellowship Bible Church,*
Rogers, Arkansas
Individual: *Lamar Steiger*

Some folks are simply made for the business of generosity. Doing generosity well is part of their God-given wiring, embedded in their thoughts and actions. And for some, it's even a part of their family heritage. Lamar Steiger is one of these people.

Lamar's grandfather was a wealthy rug manufacturer who sold his business in the 1950s and spent the rest of his life giving away and raising money for worthy causes.

Political and denominational affiliations didn't matter—if the cause was worthy, Grandfather Steiger would "twist some arms." Watching these bold pleas for generosity up close formed in Lamar what he calls a "generous gene," an impulse that says, "If we really believe what we say we believe, we should fund it. Otherwise, all the great study, deep strategic thinking, theological details, and debates are somewhat like a merry-go-round—all hat, no cattle!"

Lamar now serves as director of resource development at Fellowship Bible Church, and under his leadership the church has seen a dramatic increase in giving. Individuals and families are not only giving more but are also giving in new ways, including legacy gifts. Churches and nonprofits, in particular, should always be on the lookout for specially wired individuals like Lamar. When you find them, hire them and let them take your business of generosity to another level.

7. **Make sure you are employing the best practices for generosity.** You might have to get an education. Send a staff member to the Lilly Family School of Philanthropy at Indiana University for the "Harvard" of training in this arena. Find a church that is innovative and further down the road, and glean some wisdom from them. Remember, other folks are already doing this well. You don't have to start everything from scratch.

Generosity Snapshot: Generosity Gets Creative

Organization: *New Heights Church, Fayetteville, Arkansas*
Individual: *Jim Hall*

Jim Hall isn't just a pastor; he's also a trained mediator. So it makes sense that he's more than willing to work with people who aren't members of his church.

New Heights was overflowing its worship space at the local Boys and Girls Club, so when the club wanted to add a gym to its building, Jim led the charge for the church to share the costs. In the end, the church contributed over $3 million to fund an expansion of the club—essentially a $3 million donation, since the church doesn't own the property. While the church will get major benefit out of the deal, one of the driving factors for Jim was that the expansion would be used seven days a week by children and youth in the community. To Jim, that usage was far better than something the church owned outright but only used once or twice a week.

In this case, generosity was a win-win, but Jim and New Heights took the first sacrificial step.

CONVERSATION PARTNERS AND CONTRIBUTORS

Thanks to the following individuals for helping me think through this topic. Each has a unique voice needing to be heard regarding generosity. Collectively, their experience and wisdom are simply remarkable. Thank you for your life and labor and the willingness to be generous with it.

Tom Addington is founder and CEO of Givington's, an online shopping portal that channels 50% of the gross profit from every transaction to a non-profit cause designated by the customer (*givingtons.com*). He is also the co-founder and CEO of Brand Villages, a strategy consulting group. Tom holds a Ph.D. in communication and has served on the faculties of Pennsylvania State University and the University of Arkansas, teaching organizational design, development, culture, and communication. He has authored numerous books on leadership and serves on a number of boards. He lives in Northwest Arkansas.

Dave Anderson is a leading social entrepreneur focused on identifying innovative solutions to social problems that have the potential to change patterns across society through the use of compassion, creativity, and collaboration. He is the founder of Safe Families for Children and YouShare, and he is the executive director of Lydia Home (*safefamiliesforchildren.com, youshare.org, lydiahome.org*). In addition, Dave is a child and family psychologist with over twenty years of experience. He lives in Chicago.

Neil Bellefeuille is the co-founder and CEO of The Paradigm Project (*theparadigmproject.org*). Prior to that, he was a management and marketing consultant leading teams in the creation of brands and business units for Fortune 500 clients, including Nike, PepsiCo, and Conoco-Phillips. He lives in Colorado Springs.

Dave Blanchard is passionate about encouraging Christian-led entrepreneurship that has a positive impact on society. To this end, he co-founded and leads Praxis, which operates the Praxis Accelerators, equipping leaders from 24 early-stage businesses and nonprofits each year, and Praxis Academy, a program for undergraduates focused on the intersection of faith, culture, and startups. Previously, Dave worked at design and innovation firm IDEO and founded two companies in music and technology. He has a BA from Babson, an MBA and MEM from Northwestern, and lives in Manhattan, where he is part of the Trinity Grace Church community.

Robin Weekley Bruce is CEO of the Acton School of Business (*www.actonmba.org*), an MBA program preparing students for principled entrepreneurship. Previously, she was the founder and CEO of Be.cause Consulting and worked at Edelman Worldwide (one of the leaders in the conversation of sustainable and effective generosity) in New York. She lives in Austin, Texas.

David Dillon is a co-founder and senior managing director of the Dillon Kane Group (*dillonkane.com*), an innovation advisory and business incubation firm based in Chicago. Through his career, David led the Venture Capital business unit at Citadel Investment Group, served as the chief technology officer at Chicago Research and Trading, and as a senior vice president at Nations Bank/Bank of America building technology solutions for the Corporate Bank. He is a personal investor in various social ventures and sits on multiple boards. He lives in the Chicago area with his wife, Michele, and has two grown daughters, Lauren and Caroline.

Matthew Emerzian is the founder and CEO of Every Monday Matters, a California-based nonprofit challenging individuals, businesses, schools, and organizations to change the world ... one Monday, one action at a time (*everymondaymatters.com*). After earning an MBA from UCLA, Matthew spent ten years in the music and entertainment business in Los Angeles working with many of the biggest artists in the world. Every Monday Matters, the organization, was born from the inspiration of his book, *Every Monday Matters - 52 Ways to Make a Difference*. Matthew wholeheartedly believes that "people matter" and that, together, we can change the world. He currently lives in Los Angeles with his wife, Patty.

Alan Gotthardt is managing director and chief investment officer of TriniD Capital, a private investment company based in Atlanta. Formerly the president of Brightworth, he has been recognized in Robb Report Worth magazine as one of the Nation's 100 Most Exclusive Wealth Advisors. Alan is the author of a book on faith-based philanthropy titled *The Eternity Portfolio*, and he serves as a board member or strategic advisor to a number of nonprofit organizations.

Tyler Green is the Millennial grandson of the founder of the craft retailer Hobby Lobby. He is grateful of his upbringing and hopes to build on that heritage of generosity, impact, and service. His family, along with his studies at Indiana Wesleyan University in business and international community development, helped spur his own heart of generosity and vision for the world. He currently serves as ministries coordinator at Hobby Lobby and is on an every-day journey of personal and professional learning and growth.

Peter Greer is president and chief executive officer of HOPE International, a global microfinance organization focused on physical and spiritual poverty (*hopeinternational.org*). He is a blogger (*peterkgreer.com*) and coauthor of *The Poor Will Be Glad*, *The Spiritual Danger of Doing Good*, and *Mission Drift*. Peter lives in Lancaster, Pennsylvania.

Jim Hall is a co-directional leader and teaching pastor at New Heights Church in Fayetteville, Arkansas, one of the fastest growing churches in the state, and a leader in innovative ways to impact the local community and the world through the evangelical faith (*newheightschurch.com*). He has served on the staff of multiple churches while also working as an attorney and a licensed mediator. He lives in Northwest Arkansas.

Daniel Harrell is senior minister at Colonial Church in Edina, Minnesota (*colonialchurch.org*), following a quarter century as a minister at Park Street Church in Boston. In addition to other degrees, he holds a Ph.D. in developmental psychology. Daniel's entrepreneurial wiring, heart for the streets, and commitment to effective church practice helped launch the Innove project in the Twin Cities. He is the author of a number of books all touching the intersection of putting one's faith to work. He lives in Minneapolis.

Daryl Heald began his career as a commercial real estate broker in Atlanta, GA, then in 1997 joined the Maclellan Foundation. While at Maclellan, Heald helped launch: Generous Giving, Giving Wisely, and Global Generosity. Most of his time now is spent in speaking and encouraging business people in the global financial capitals to be generous. He is also actively investing in private equity deals with a particular emphasis on businesses with social impact. Daryl currently serves on ten boards in both the for-profit and not-for-profit arenas. Some of his favorite pastimes include golfing, fly-fishing, and barbequing. Heald holds a BS degree in economics from Westmont College, and he and his wife, Cathy, reside in Lookout Mountain, GA, and have eight children.

Henry Ho is the co-founder of NorthStar Partnering Group and the chief business development officer and co-founder of Field Agent, a 2009 start-up that leverages crowdsourcing and smartphone technologies to give companies real-time access to information and insights (*fieldagent. net*). Henry spent two decades with Procter & Gamble, including six years as their Wal-Mart Asia team leader and country manager of Procter & Gamble Hong Kong. He has led, and continues to lead, multiple start-ups in addition to Field Agent. He lives in Northwest Arkansas.

Peb Jackson is the principal of the Jackson Consulting Group working on projects with private sector and nonprofit organizations relative to maximizing opportunities and developing leaders. He has worked in the social issues arena for several decades, including stints as the senior vice president of Focus on the Family, executive vice president of Generous Giving, vice president of global initiatives with Saddleback Church/ Purpose Driven Ministries, the founder of the Legacy Group, and an active participant in the Obama administration's Office of Faith-Based and Community Initiative. He serves on multiple boards and advisory groups, ranging from the Yale Center for Faith & Culture to CURE International. He lives in Colorado Springs.

Josh Kwan is the director of international giving for the David Weekley Family Foundation, where he helps provide growth capital to a portfolio of young nonprofits tackling global poverty. His contributions to these organizations include strategic planning, financial assessment, and serving on the board of directors. He is also the co-founder and chairman of Praxis, a nonprofit that helps entrepreneurs build high-impact organizations, and a co-founder of Carpenters, a company that creates mobile apps for spiritual disciplines. Josh graduated from Harvard College and Northwestern University's Kellogg School of Management. He lives near San Francisco.

Kevin McCollum is the executive director of Lightbearers (*lightbearersconnects.com*), a nonprofit providing renewable funding for Christian missions in Asia and northern Africa. Lightbearers converts apartment complexes near U.S. college campuses into discipleship communities and funds mission work with the profits. Kevin has an array of ministry and professional experiences ranging from business development to "non-profit leadership". He lives in Northwest Arkansas.

Tyler Merrick is a social entrepreneur and founder of Project 7 (*project7. com*). This consumer goods company making everyday products gives back to seven areas for good around the globe. The seven areas are: Feed the Hungry, Heal the Sick, Hope for Peace, House the Homeless, Quench the Thirsty, Teach Them Well, and Save the Earth. His company was one of the early leaders in baking profit sharing into their company success formula. Since 2008, Project 7 has grown to become a nationwide distributor serving various companies like Caribou Coffee, Forever 21, Babies R Us, convenience stores, specialty grocery stores, and American Airlines to name a few. He lives in Orange County, California.

David and **Mel Murray** are the founders of a pair of social impact companies in northern India—JOYN and Dehradun Guitar Company (*joynindia.com, dehradunguitars.com*). After a decade in sales and marketing, they moved to India with a passion to connect artisans to markets while impacting change in the spiritual lives of those artisans. JOYN produces handmade products, and Dehradun Guitar Company produces handcrafted acoustic guitars. They live in Rajpur, India.

Scott Page is the vice president of people and culture for CCF Brands (*ccfbrands.com*), a value-leading consumer foods company specializing in eggs. Scott leads the company in initiatives that help employees live the company's values, appreciate one another, and impact their community. For years Scott has been a leader in the faith and justice community, including more than a decade as a pastor and his current service on the board of the Cobblestone Project. He lives in Northwest Arkansas.

Mike Rusch is chief operating officer of Pure Charity (*mikerusch.org, purecharity.com*), a nonprofit organization making it possible to leverage everyday spending and allowing consumers to support causes and organizations that matter most to them. Previously, Mike worked in the field of shopper insights and analytics with leading Fortune 100 companies, including Disney and Nickelodeon. He lives in Northwest Arkansas.

Tara Russell is founder and chief executive officer of Create Common Good (*createcommongood.org*), a social + entrepreneurial venture serving the marginalized. Tara has worked internationally for Fortune 500 companies and NGOs. Her work spans process engineering at General Motors in Shanghai, technical sales and marketing at Intel, and product development at Nike. Tara co-founded NightLight International, an organization serving women at risk in Bangkok, Thailand. She lives in Boise, Idaho.

Steve Shadrach has spent his life mobilizing college students to serve around the globe. He has founded, led, or worked closely with organizations such as Student Mobilization, The Traveling Team, and the Center for Mission Mobilization. He also served for eight years as the director of mobilization for the U.S. Center for World Mission. Steve has dedicated much of his energy to the area of raising funds. The last of his four books addresses this very topic: *The God Ask: A Fresh, Biblical Approach to Personal Support Raising.* Steve lives in Fayetteville, Arkansas.

Jeff Shinabarger is a social entrepreneur and author of *More or Less: Choosing a Lifestyle of Excessive Generosity*. Jeff has a vision to make Atlanta a center for social innovation and has personally engaged in over 100 start-ups solving problems. His work has been featured by *CNN, USA Weekend, Atlanta Journal Constitution, Huffington Post, Christianity Today, Coca-Cola, Relevant Magazine*, and *Chicago Sun Times*. Jeff serves as creative advisor to Epoch Missions Gala and the Chick-fil-A Environmental Stewardship Committee. Jeff and his wife, Andre, live in East Atlanta Village and have two children and a boxer named Max.

Greg Spencer is co-founder and chairman of The Paradigm Project (*theparadigmproject.org*). He is also the former president of the Blue Source companies and spent twenty years working in corporate mergers and acquisitions, law, capital markets, and environmental and operational risk management. He lives in Park City, Utah.

Lamar Stieger is the director of resource development of Fellowship Bible Church, Rogers, Arkansas (*fellowshipnwa.org*). After more than a decade as the general manager of JACS Ranch, and more than a decade as a community pastor, Lamar took on his current position with one of the five largest churches in the state. He lives in Northwest Arkansas.

Justin Whaley serves as chief executive officer of CCF Brands (*ccfbrands. com*). As the second-generation leader Justin is passionate about staying true to the legacy his father built, all while guiding the company forward into even more territories of growth and leadership. He has a particular interest in exploring the edges of the gospel application into the fabric of business. He lives in Northwest Arkansas.

CCF Brands Partnership
A special thanks to **Justin Whaley, Scott Page,** and the entire CCF Brands team for leaning into this project with extraordinary generosity. Their curiosity for the subject and their longing to blend generosity into their core business model is contagious.

NOTES

1. Laura Arrillaga-Andreesen, *Giving 2.0: Transform Your Giving and Our World* (San Francisco: Jossey-Bass, 2012), 128; and Howard G. Buffett, *40 Chances: Finding Hope in a Hungry World* (New York: Simon & Schuster, 2013).

2. "Generation G," Trend Watching, February 2009, http://trendwatching.com/trends/generationg/.

3. "What Is Generosity?" University of Notre Dame, http://generosityresearch.nd.edu/more-about-the-initiative/what-is-generosity/.

4. Muhammad Yunus, *Banker to the Poor: Micro-Lending and the Battle Against World Poverty* (New York: PublicAffairs, 1999), 237.

5. Shawn Parr, "Why Every Monday Matters," Fast Company, April 9, 2012, http://www.fastcompany.com/1829978/why-every-monday-matters.

6. Matthew Emerzian and Kelly Bozza, *Every Monday Matters: 52 Ways to Make a Difference* (Nashville: Thomas Nelson, 2008). See also everymondaymatters.com.

7. Volunteering and Civic Life in America, http://www.volunteeringinamerica.gov/. According to one study, the level of Americans' participation in giving and volunteering is enough to make the United States rank near, but not at, the top of the list of the world's most generous nations. "World Giving Index 2012," Charities Aid Foundation, December 2012, http://www.cafonline.org/PDF/WorldGivingIndex2012WEB.pdf.

8. "Charitable Giving Statistics," National Philanthropic Trust, http://www.nptrust.org/philanthropic-resources/charitable-giving-statistics.

9. Sasha Dichter, "The Generosity Experiment," TED Blog, http://vimeo.com/29140232.

10. Augustine, *City of God*, book 9.

11. Rachael Chong, "How Do You Develop a Brand Around Doing Good Business?" Fast Company, June 6, 2013, http://www.fastcoexist.com/1682250/how-do-you-develop-a-brand-around-doing-good-business.

12. Timothy Keller, *Counterfeit Gods: The Empty Promises of Money, Sex, and Power, and the Only Hope That Matters* (New York: Dutton, 2009), 52.

13. Basil the Great, quoted at Orthodox Diakonia, http://www.iocc.org/orthodoxdiakonia/index.php?id=p3.

14. "The Millennial Impact Report 2012," http://cdn.trustedpartner.com/docs/library/AchieveMCON2013/TheMillennialImpactReport2012.pdf.

15. "Generation G," Trend Watching, February 2009, http://trendwatching.com/trends/generationg/.

16. Tyson Foods, http://www.tysonsustainability.com/.

17. Bill and Melinda Gates pledge letter, Giving Pledge, http://givingpledge.org/pdf/letters/Gates_Letter.pdf.

18. Eric Friedman, *Reinventing Philanthropy: A Framework for More Effective Giving* (Washington, DC: Potomac Books, 2013).

19. "The Growth of Cause Marketing," Cause Marketing Forum, http://www.causemarketingforum.com/site/c.bkLUKcOTLkK4E/b.6412299/apps/s/content.asp?ct=8965443.

20. I am grateful to Sean DeWitt for identifying these three messages for me.

21. Michael E. Porter and Mark R. Cramer, "The Competitive Advantage of Corporate Philanthropy," *Harvard Business Review*, December 2002, http://hbr.org/2002/12/the-competitive-advantage-of-corporate-philanthropy/ar/1.

22. Brett J. Blackledge, "Some 9/11 Charities Failed Miserably," Associated Press, August 25, 2011, http://news.yahoo.com/ap-impact-9-11-charities-failed-miserably-090944197.html.

23. The Center for Investigative Reporting, http://cironline.org/americasworstcharities; and *Tampa Bay Times*, http://www.tampabay.com/americas-worst-charities/.

24. Associated Press, "Hundreds of Suicides in India Linked to Microfinance Organizations," February 24, 2012, http://www.businessinsider.com/hundreds-of-suicides-in-india-linked-to-microfinance-organizations-2012-2.

25. Some of the following material reflects Johanna Neuman, "The Distinctly American Tradition of Charity," *U.S. News & World Report*, October 18, 2010, http://www.usnews.com/news/articles/2010/10/18/the-distinctly-american-tradition-of-charity. See also Lawrence J. Friedman and Mark D. McGarvie, *Charity, Philanthropy, and Civility in American History* (Cambridge, UK: Cambridge University Press, 2004). For a twentieth-century history, see Olivier Zunz, *Philanthropy in America: A History* (Princeton, NJ: Princeton University Press, 2011). For a study of business generosity, see Archie B. Carroll and others, *Corporate Responsibility: The American Experience* (Cambridge, UK: Cambridge University Press, 2012).

26. John Winthrop, "A Modell of Christian Charity (1630)," http://history.hanover.edu/texts/winthmod.html.

27. Giving Institute, "Giving USA Report 2013: The Annual Report on Philanthropy for the Year 2012," http://www.givingusareports.org/. Governments are also sources of money for social good through such things as funding schools, providing disaster relief, and giving foreign aid grants. In fact, the sums involved dwarf those from any other source of giving. But it's no simple thing to determine which parts of government budgets actually constitute generosity and which don't. Consequently, government giving is not included in this or similar reports.

28. Milton Friedman, "The Social Responsibility of Business Is to Increase Its Profits," *New York Times Magazine*, September 13, 1970, http://www.colorado.edu/studentgroups/libertarians/issues/friedman-soc-

resp-business.html. See also Justin Fox, "The Social Responsibility Is to Increase…What Exactly?" *HBR Blog Network*, April 18, 2012, http://blogs.hbr.org/2012/04/you-might-disagree-with-milton/.

29. Quoted in Margaret Coady, "The Case for CSR: The CEO Perspective," *CECP*, August 25, 2010, http://cecp.co/press-room/cecp-blog/1004-the-case-for-csr-the-ceo-perspective.html.

30. John Mackey and Raj Sisodia, *Conscious Capitalism: Liberating the Historic Spirit of Business* (Boston: Harvard Business School Publishing, 2013), 26.

31. Coca-Cola, http://www.coca-colacompany.com/stories/corporate-giving.

32. "How America's Biggest Companies Give," *Chronicle of Philanthropy*, July 14, 2013, http://philanthropy.com/article/How-America-s-Biggest/140269/.

33. Statistic from the Center on Nonprofits and Philanthropy (http://www.urban.org/center/cnp//). Cited in Richard Tait, "The Importance of Earned Income in Your Funding Model," *Stanford Social Innovation Review*, November 7, 2011, http://www.ssireview.org/blog/entry/the_importance_of_earned_income_in_your_funding_model.

34. William Foster and Jeffrey Bradach, "Should Nonprofits Seek Profits?" *Harvard Business Review*, February 2005, http://hbr.org/2005/02/should-nonprofits-seek-profits/ar/1.

35. Dan Pallotta, *Uncharitable: How Restraints on Nonprofits Undermine Their Potential* (Medford, MA: Tufts University Press, 2008). See also Dan Pallotta, "The Way We Think About Charity Is Dead Wrong," *TED*, March 2013, http://www.ted.com/talks/dan_pallotta_the_way_we_think_about_charity_is_dead_wrong.html.

36. See Generous Church, generouschurch.com.

37. "Multiple Bottom Line Profit," *Nehemiah Project*, January 11, 2012, http://nehemiahproject.org/be-devotionals/multiple-bottom-line-profit/.

38. "AT&T TOMS Shoes," http://www.youtube.com/watch?v=Ay7xrXBa7Zo.

39. C. S. Lewis, *The Four Loves* (New York: Harcourt, Brace, 1960), 50.

40. "Our Principles in Action: Summary 2012," Mars, http://www.mars.com/global/assets/doc/pia_exec_2012/Mars_PIA_Highlights_2012_EN_report.pdf.

41. "The Global, Socially Conscious Consumer," Nielsen, March 27, 2012, http://www.nielsen.com/us/en/newswire/2012/the-global-socially-conscious-consumer.html.

42. Ibid.

43. "Edelman Goodpurpose 2012" executive summary, goodpurpose, 3, http://purpose.edelman.com/.

44. Michael E. Porter and Mark R. Kramer, "Creating Shared Value," *Harvard Business Review*, January 2011, http://hbr.org/2011/01/the-big-idea-creating-shared-value.

45. Jim Collins, *Good to Great: Why Some Companies Make the Leap—and Others Don't* (New York: HarperBusiness, 2001), 194.

46. Lauren Bush Lauren, interview with Donna Fenn, "Lauren Bush Lauren: Fashioning a Social Enterprise," *Inc.*, http://www.inc.com/donna-fenn/lauren-bush-lauren-feed-fashioning-social-enterprise.html.

47. Brent Freeman, "5 Companies that Make Money and Do Good," *Inc.*, August 16, 2012, http://www.inc.com/brent-freeman/social-entrepreneurs-5-great-companies-that-make-money-and-do-good_1.html/1.

48. Stephen R. Graves, "Everything Has Overhead," December 16, 2013, http://www.stephenrgraves.com/everything-has-overhead/.

49. Milton Friedman, "The Social Responsibility of Business Is to Increase Its Profits," *New York Times Magazine*, September 13, 1970, http://www.colorado.edu/studentgroups/libertarians/issues/friedman-soc-resp-business.html.

50. Peter Greer and Chris Horst, *Mission Drift: The Unspoken Crisis Facing Leaders, Charities, and Churches* (Minneapolis: Bethany House, 2014), 15.

51. Jim Collins, *How the Mighty Fall: And Why Some Companies Never Give In* (New York: Jim Collins, 2009).

52. If you need help with solidifying your mission, check out the step-by-step process in Steve Graves and others, *From Concept to Scale: Creating a Gospel-Minded Organization* (Praxis Media, 2013).

53. "Declaration of Interdependence," Whole Foods Market, http://www.wholefoodsmarket.com/mission-values/core-values/declaration-interdependence.

54. John Mackey and Raj Sisodia, *Conscious Capitalism: Liberating the Historic Spirit of Business* (Boston: Harvard Business School Publishing, 2013).

55. "Meet Malti," Light the World, http://www.lighttheworld.co/malti.

56. "Street Smart," Aasraa Trust, http://aasraatrust.org/street-smart-project-for-street-children/.

57. JOYN, http://joynindia.com/.

58. Dehradun Guitar Company, http://dehradunguitars.com/.

59. Elizabeth Blair, "Charity Watchdog Shakes Up Ratings to Focus on Results," NPR, October 22, 2013, http://www.npr.org/2013/10/22/236392607/charity-watchdog-shakes-up-ratings-to-focus-on-results.

60. Laura Arrillaga-Andreesen, *Giving 2.0: Transform Your Giving and Our World* (San Francisco: Jossey-Bass, 2012), 15–16.

61. Kris Frieswick, "Ex-Cons Relaunching Lives as Entrepreneurs," *Inc.*, May 29, 2012, http://www.inc.com/magazine/201206/kris-frieswick/catherine-rohr-defy-ventures-story-of-redemption.html.

Other titles from Stephen R. Graves:

Steve is the founder of Coaching by Cornerstone, where he advises executives, business owners, and young entrepreneurs. When he isn't working his day job (or fishing), Steve writes and speaks often on topics related to strategy, work, and faith. After publishing the *Life@Work Magazine* some years ago, Steve recently launched a new writing and publishing venture, *stephenrgraves.com*. Through this venture, Steve is helping to stage conversations and create content around four themes he is passionate about: organizational strategy, social innovation, leadership development, and practical faith. To learn more, check out his weekly blog and look for the next book coming out soon.

———————————————

For more resources from KJK Inc. Publishing, go to *stephenrgraves.com.*

Notes

Notes

Notes

Notes

Notes